Brian O'Nolan wrote under the p
Myles na Gopaleen. He was born
of Dublin, he graduated from Un
career as a student (editing a maga
Civil Service, in which he eventua
died in Dublin on 1 April 1966. His
The Dalkey Archive, The Third Police...., ... *The Poor Mouth* (originally published in Irish as *An Béal Bocht*).

By the same author

The Third Policeman
At Swim-Two-Birds
The Hard Life
The Poor Mouth
The Dalkey Archive
Stories and Plays
The Various Lives of Keats and Chapman and *The Brother*
Further Cuttings from Cruiskeen Lawn
The Best of Myles
Myles Away from Dublin
Myles Before Myles

FLANN O'BRIEN
(Myles na Gopaleen)

The Hair of the Dogma

A further selection from 'Cruiskeen Lawn'

Edited and with a Preface by Kevin O'Nolan

PALADIN
GRAFTON BOOKS
A Division of the Collins Publishing Group

LONDON GLASGOW
TORONTO SYDNEY AUCKLAND

Paladin
Grafton Books
A Division of the Collins Publishing Group
8 Grafton Street, London W1X 3LA

Published in Paladin Books 1989

First published in Great Britain by
Hart-Davis, MacGibbon Ltd 1977
Reissued by Grafton Books 1987

Copyright © Evelyn O'Nolan 1977

ISBN 0-586-08947-0

Printed and bound in Great Britain by
Collins, Glasgow

Set in Times

Acknowledgements

The publishers would like to express their thanks to Kevin O'Nolan, the Editor, and to the Proprietors of the *Irish Times*, in whose pages the contents of this book originally appeared, for their co-operation and help.

Contents

Preface

This third volume of selections from 'Cruiskeen Lawn', Myles na Gopaleen's column in the *Irish Times*, covers as does its companion, *Further Cuttings from Cruiskeen Lawn*, roughly the period from 1947 to 1957, though some earlier and later pieces are included. As in *The Best of Myles*, some attempt has been made to classify pieces under various heads for the convenience of readers. Through half its history the column appeared under the name 'Cruiskeen Lawn' (Full Jug), without further clue as to what readers were actually having on any particular day. However, from about 1953 the author entitled each piece, and the heading 'Cruiskeen Lawn', with the author's pen-name, was transferred to a box in the body of the column. Accordingly, in the present selection no attempt has been made to classify separately these captioned pieces, but they are all put together, each with its own heading, in the section 'Titled Pieces', the largest section in the book.

The first column of 'Cruiskeen Lawn' was published on 4 October 1940. It appeared on the leader page of the *Irish Times*. Characteristically it was an attack on a leading article which had appeared in the *Irish Times* of 28 September. The article, under 'Cruiskeen Lawn', was headed 'From a Correspondent', and was subscribed 'An Broc' (i.e. The Badger). Before the next appearance of the column on 13 October, the author had hit upon his final and most lasting pseudonym, Myles na gCopaleen.

In the succeeding weeks the frequent appearance of the column, mostly in Irish, led readers to wonder what had got into the *Irish Times* – something not quite healthy, to judge by some of the hostile letters which readers began to send in. But letters of approval began to appear too. In a short time the column was an accepted feature of the leader page.

This was its home for a long time. The author, from his sanctuary, often hurled abuse and criticism at his editor, R. M. Smyllie, across the thin line which divided his territory

from the editorial column. Even as late as July 1951 he was
writing:

Not the least of my duties is keeping an eye on the Editor of this
newspaper and rebutting, for the benefit of our simpler readers,
the various heresies propounded in his leading articles. Saturday's
article was a great shock to me.

Alec Newman, who later became editor, was at that time
writing 'Irishman's Diary' under the pseudonym Quidnunc.
He considered it unseemly that 'Cruiskeen Lawn' should
appear on the editorial page and strenuously objected. But
such objections fell on deaf ears. Later the column was moved
to a safe distance on another page.

   In the early days of the column Myles was also engaged on
a satirical novel in Irish called *An Béal Bocht*. Readers may
be interested in an article which appeared in 'Cruiskeen
Lawn' ten years later on the subject of that book's publication. The article is reprinted here, the first item in the
section 'From Day to Day'.

                                                   Kevin O'Nolan

The Irish

A point which I noticed was not emphasised at the Celtic Congress was the *precision* of the Irish language. Therein is the secret why Irish cannot be revived; the present age shrinks from precision and 'understands' only soft woolly words which have really no particular meaning, like 'cultural heritage' or 'the exigent dictates of modern traffic needs'. The Latin *scribo*, for example, means 'I scratch' but the same word is used to denote the meaning 'I write, I draw'. What does the phrase *equum scribo* mean? It could mean 'I draw a horse, as in a sweepstake'. Or it could mean 'I scratch a horse because he is itchy'. Or 'I scratch a horse, because he is lame and will not win'. Or 'I draw a horse (sketch)'. Not much precision there, you will agree. Now the Irish take this word *scribo* for their roan, pardon, for their own but they throw out all this damn ambiguity. The Irish word *scribim* means 'I scratch' and nothing else, while *scriobhaim* means 'I write' and nothing else. (Just what does the English word 'scribble' mean? Don't answer – your 'explanation' will be just as vague!)

When you consider the awkward, stiff, self-conscious and 'literary' stuff that was written by Chaucer – *and so recently!* – and compare it with Irish poetry written by me one thousand years before Chaucer was born, you will inevitably reflect upon the ludicrous pretensions of the jerry-built brand-new limey civilisation and 'literature' you are so urgently begged to admire by the Editor of the *Irish Times* (a Mason, by the way!). You may also bring to mind the noble, proud and scornful words of the seventeenth-century Aodhagán O Rathaille:

> *Rachadsa a h-aithle searc*
> *na laoch don chill,*
> *Na flatha fá raibh mo shean*
> *roimth éag do Chríost.*

Let me now quote a little poem I scratched – sorry! – I

wrote myself at least a thousand years ago. That would be, of course, before Jurtheim, the German pedant. Observe, I ask, the felicity, the freshness – above all, the *humanity* – of these following little verses:

> *Sgíth mo chrob ón sgríbinn*
> *ní dígainn mo glés géroll,*
> *sgeithid mo phenn gulban-caolta*
> *digh daolta do dub glégorm.*

Now is not that fine? See the old monk, weary, but good-humoured? He sighs and shakes his head, but writes on. Why? Listen again:

> *Bruinnidh sruaim n-ecna nDé*
> > *fhinn*
> *as mo láim degduinn desmais,*
> *doirtidh a digh for duillinn*
> *do dubh in chuilinn chnesglais.*

Well lads? Good or bad? See that berry? See how it glistens, holly berry of the green epidermis! By the gob you can't deny it. I could write in those days, aye, and write about writing without being a bore, like Seamus. Here's the last verse:

> *Sínidh mo phenn beg braonach*
> *tar aonach lebor lígoll,*
> *gan sgor fri selba segann,*
> *dian sgíth mo chrob ón sgríbunn*

By Gor! Did Bernard Shaw himself put pen to paper with better effect 'the best day he was in it', as they say in Irish? Could, say, Frank Lemass of C.I.E. write as fine a poem as that? (If he could he's a most affected man to refrain from writing poetry.) Could Hone attempt the task? Father Gannon, S.J.? Willy Dwyer? The Manager of the M. and L. in Terenure? Faugh!!!

Perhaps I'd better translate the poem for the benefit of limey visitors who are over here drinking the malt intended by Providence for our good selves. Here goes:

> My hand has a pain from writing,
> Not steady the sharp tool of my
> > craft

Its slender beak spews bright
    ink –
A beetle-dark shining draught.

Streams of the wisdom of white
    God
From my fair-brown, fine hand
    sally,
On the page they splash their
    flood
In ink of the green-skinned holly.

My little dribbly pen stretches
Across the great white paper
    plain,
Insatiable for splendid riches –
That is why my hand has a pain!

Anybody who thinks that isn't excellent must be mad! I wrote the original in an age nearer to that of Horace than to this, yet it could have been written yesterday. Which, of course, is the test of true art. (Never let me hear you use a phrase like 'modern art'.) It is indeed a very fine, engaging, handsome poem. See the humorous juxtaposition of *gulban* and *daolta* – the contrast as between the bird-beak swallowing beetles and the pen-beak spewing beetles, black beetle-like words on the page! Witty? Surrealist? I should think so!

Would any reader who knows a grander person than my Excellency please communicate with the Editor of the *Irish Times*?

* * *

You have a lot of chat out of you from time to time about 'the priceless heritage of our Gaelic past', 'our national language' and so on but so far as I can see, ye are doing very little to bring the old native civilisation back. I wonder are ye in earnest at all? Beyond the earnest lip-service ye pay to Irish (here I mean *Irish Malt* and I don't exclude those visiting doctors) I can't think of a single thing that has been done to bring back *an seana-shaol*. Take the political organisation of society. The ancient native order was patriarchal and aristocratic, the people knew their place (i.e. the scullery) and 'democracy', God help us, was unheard of. The administration of law was speedy and simple, because only a handful of people had 'rights'. An exclusive caste of poets discharged the functions of commentator and recorder, and these men acknowledged *no one* as their superiors. They were maintained in great luxury and treated with the reverence and circumspection that are reserved for those who are feared, for they could ruin a man with a poisonous couplet. They were the journalists of their day, and they had a traditional right to libel whom they pleased. What is the position of the journalist today? Let it suffice to say that in my own case, when I go out for a walk (of an evening) I deem it wiser to go disguised as a man!

These speculations were brought into my mind by an encouraging note which appeared in a June issue of the *Irish Builder and Engineer*, dealing with the erection of churches:

At the annual meeting of the Royal Society of Ulster Architects in Belfast, the subject of the founding of a Choir of Architecture at Queen's University was mentioned by the President, Mr R. H. Gibson . . .

A choir suggests monks, and monks suggest beautiful medieval architecture such as the abbey at Timoleague, planned and built with limestone, sand and bullocks' blood by monkish hands. Why should it have to be left to Mr Gibson of Belfast to suggest so venerable an alternative to the shams and affectations of present-day architects (whom I recently dealt with so delightfully)?

You can't revive Gaelic civilisation overnight but you *can* reassemble it piecemeal. Reinstate journalists in their ancient office of privilege, re-entrust the building arts to monks, and you have made a beginning. Then proceed to revive the various Gaelic *fonctionnaires* who have been permitted to disappear completely in the shabby secondhand conditions of today. Opportunities exist on every hand. For example, the arrangements in your hotels are bad copies of those in foreign hotels, with a boots, porter, 'office' and so on. Meals are not ready for you at the times you specify, and you frequently find a retired bank manager from Cardiff asleep in your bed when you leave the bar at 4 a.m. No large establishment in the old days would dare to exist without a *Taoiseach Teaghlaigh*, or Household Captain. The old tale

Bruighen Da Derga gives you some idea of his standing and duties:

> I saw there a bed and one man in it. Coarse hair upon him. Though a dish of wild apples had been cast upon his hair, not an apple of them would fall to the ground, but each apple would stick upon its own separate hair. His high-priced cloak about him in the house. Every controversy which occurs in the house about a seat or a bed, it is to his decision they all come. If a needle should drop in the house its fall would be heard when he speaks. A great black pole over him. It is like the shaft of a mill with its wings, and its head-cogs, and its points. Dost thou know the like of him? That man is Tuidle of Ulster, the Captain of Conaire's household. There is no annulling the decision of that man. A man who regulates seats, and beds, and food, for everyone. It is his Household-pole that stands over him.

Such an essential type of man simply does not exist now. How many Irishmen can boast even of a household-pole today? Probably not a dozen in the whole country. I don't believe there is one in the much-vaunted National Museum.

I think it would be quite simple to revive the Household Captain, with his own household-pole complete with wings, head-cogs and points. He may appear a bit archaic but so also, I suppose, is the notion that it should be somebody's business to look after beds and food. (Even in English I think the word 'food', in its true sense, is nearly obsolete; nowadays people have 'bites', 'snacks' or 'tea' at a 'buffet' or 'canteen'; anything horizontal is a 'bed'.)

Tell you what might be a more popular choice. How about reviving the historic Irish maiden? Your ancient saga *Táin Bó Cuailgne*, or *The Cattle-Spoil of Cooley*, gives a fairly detailed description of this lady – the sort of thing the Guards would circulate if she was 'wanted'. Surely the following does not quite describe your wife? –

Thus was the maiden, and a sword in her right hand, with its seven joints of red gold in its points. A speckle-spotted green cloak about her. A bushy, heavy-headed brooch in the cloak over her breast. A crimson, rich-blooded countenance with her. A blue, laughing eye with her. Lips red, thin. Teeth shining, pearly: it would seem to you that they were showers of fair pearls that had been cast into her head. As sweet as the strings of triangular harps, a-playing by the hands of true professors, were the sweet sound of her voice and her charming words. As white as snow shed during one night, was the lustre of her skin, and her body appearing through her robe outside. Feet thin, long, white. Nails crimson, regular, circular, sharp, with her. Hair fair-yellow, gold-shining, upon her. Three locks of her hair turned round her head; another lock shading her down to the calves of her legs.

And phwat is wrong with that, may I ask? Is what you have today . . . an improvement? Which would make the better film star – the old or the new? Let me put it this way: the Irish girl of today is just the run of the mill, whereas yesterday's girl is the run of de Mille.

*   *   *

Well, I see ye have your *Oireachtas* on again, with speeches, pipe bands, songs, story-telling and chess competitions. God speed the work, I hope it keeps fine for ye! No shadow of the atom bomb there, I'll go bail! Things went off well, if I can believe what I read in the *Irish Times*:

> The occasion of the *Oireachtas* was a very interesting one, and was a most gratifying success from almost every point of view. The hall was fully occupied, and the deepest interest was manifested in the proceedings, which, for the most part, were conducted in the Irish language. Portions of the prize compositions were read to the meeting, and the remainder of the programme consisted of musical selections. The first item was a performance of Irish airs on the Irish pipes by Mr T. Rowsome. He opened with the famous old melody, 'The Cuilfhionn', of which Handel is related to have said that he would rather have been the composer than of any of his great oratorios . . .

I forgot to say that the copy of the *Irish Times* in which *that* appeared is dated 1897; probably you guessed as much, for nobody would dare to speak of Handel like that nowadays. But here is the point: you have had your *Oireachtas* now for fifty years. Are you satisfied, from a study of the results, that it is a good act? Bless me, I believe you are!

Many years ago I had occasion to examine, at the instance of His Grace the second Duke of Argyll, that extremely odd assemblage of hagiologies, prayers, incantations, myths and poems which you claim to be your national literature and, impressed by the mystical focus of all that, admiring its hardness and elegance of language, taking note of its remoteness from the corruption of contemporary European thought, I arranged with one or two friends – John Fleming and Michael Cusack are names which come to me undimmed from the past – for the foundation, in 1881, of the Gaelic Union, the aim of which was 'the preservation and cultivation of the Irish language'. (Horrified of prolixity and discursiveness, I here make no mention of my earlier work in the Royal Irish Academy, which I founded in 1786 and wherein I was destined to give Ireland many years of selfless labour in company with O'Donovan and O'Curry, Reeves, Todd, Petrie, Stokes, McCullagh and Jellett, great men all.) This much I must make crystal clear, my aim in founding the Gaelic Union was a worthy one. I sought to preserve what was signified, urbane and adult in the remnants of the gaelic civilisation then subsisting. At no time did I authorise the revolting manifestations and exercises which go by the name of 'gaelicism' today. Nothing was further from my thoughts than a 'gaelic revival' that connoted the atrophy of Irish intellects nor did I dream that the publication of a few old tales should become a base pathogenic influence on the minds of the young and the innocent. I did not foresee that my labours should in due time lead grown men who were apparently sane to denounce many ideas and practices on the sole ground that they were 'foreign'. I did not think that ever would come the day when young Irishmen, made from the incomparable salts and essences of the Irish soil, should permit their minds to decay to the putrescent flux that has made possible the sticking up on public buildings of the statement *A Gaelic Ireland is a Prosperous Ireland*! And who will blame me if I affirm that I completely failed to see that my Gaelic Union would lead to the migration of hordes of work-shy agricultural labourers from the south-west of Ireland into Government clerkships in Dublin?

What really happened was this ... We always dealt with business matters first, and then ——

The general meeting finally resolved itself into an Irish conversation meeting, when a discussion in that language was instituted on the meaning of certain words obsolete in some parts of Ireland . . .

The business for which the meeting had been called together having been satisfactorily transacted, the meeting resolved itself into an Irish conversational one, the subject of discussion being the old weights and measures used in Ireland for farm and dairy produce . . .

The allusions (in Mr Fleming's speech) to the use of the Irish language in all the old monastery schools along with the Latin, and to the exclusion of the English, were approved of. Reference was made to the knowledge possessed by the Irish chieftains of Latin, French, Spanish and Italian, and to their ignorance at the same time of English, which was regarded in Ireland as a barbarous tongue . . .

The following were the subjects discussed in the Irish language . . . The condition of the Irish-speaking fishermen of the west coast; the necessity for encouraging the singing of Irish songs; the new features of the coming number of the *Gaelic Journal*, and the issuing of improved elementary books in Irish. Some ladies of the Irish class having joined the meeting, the discussion in Irish on the western fishing population was resumed . . .

Those were the days! But you must not think that we were namby-pamby – far from it! The old journals are packed with the most savage controversies as to the meaning of words; that most indigenous erratum, the 'mistake', is the subject of brutal letter-writing far beyond the present-day boundary of libel.

There is one other little matter that comes to my mind. The wiseacres of today think they are called upon to decide unique issues never before raised before human kind. Take this business of teaching school children through a language of which at first they know nothing. Well, the old-timers had a Royal Commission on that in the eighties. Let me quote from its report:

In what parts of the country is Irish still spoken to any considerable extent? – In the counties of Galway, Mayo, Cork, Kerry and Waterford, these are the chief. In the county of Galway 62.1 per cent of the people speak Irish.

And who prefer Irish? – They prefer it, and speak it, when they have the opportunity. Those who speak Irish and English both numbered for all Ireland 942,261, or 16.3 of the population.

The total of the Irish-speaking population is 1,105,536 or 19.1 per cent of the whole population.

Has the National Board ever made provision for teaching the people through the medium of Irish? – I am very sorry to say it has not.

What is your opinion with regard to instructing the people in Irish, with a view to their learning English? – I believe it to be next to impossible to teach, skilfully and effectively, the Irish-speaking population by the ordinary process adopted in our schools, which at once gives them the English alphabet, English books and English everything, without reference to translation into, or from, their vernacular language . . .

What practical advantage would arise from any attempt to foster and encourage the use of the Irish language in the schools? – I think we should have English more generally and speedily taught if we began by teaching the people to read in the language they speak . . .

What does this prove? Search me. The Commission did not recommend that Irish should be taught in the schools, yet where today are your million Irish-speakers? Dead? Nonsense! Well you know that that's no answer!

* * *

My poor friend James Joyce who was a great man, for a joke, (leave that comma after 'joke'!) once asked me: if a man, hacking away in fury at a block of stone, were to produce a work of art, what is the answer? I'm sure either of us cared. (Note please however that *I'm* not the one that wrote 'Yinnie Gonne's WAAC' – I only 'corrected' the proofs.)

But it goes on all the time, this accidental surgery, producing these fascinating and expensive *œuvres* and, of course, the only purpose of the thing is to show people, and artists in particular, how important they are. The old man, his technique perfected in forty years of study, practising twelve hours a day, is suddenly shamed by an eskimo, aged two, who, though illiterate, lame, deaf and suffering from a weeping affection of the eyes, can play anything with a grandeur of interpretation, with an insight too acute to be 'acquired', with a perfection that is not even to be discussed. (Worse – consider the converse: imagine a quite old man, trained in some dreadful College of Art manned by landless

crofters (I mean civil servants), suddenly painting a quite
good ... abstract job! Oh, humiliation!)

But here is a more ordinary example – ordinary, of course,
only in the sense that the vessel through which a significant
mystical message has been transmitted is but a simple paragraph heading from one of our giant dailies. (By the way, we
used to have two giant dailies, they lived in the Gloucester
Diamond and they were so big we had to raise the dining-
room table with books and sit on high stools around it so
they could serve comfortably! We have a house telephone,
of course – it's handy for them, they always ring up when it's
time for the missus to go down and get the dinner and bring
up the plates. Ah, yes.) Here's the heading I'm talking about
and take a good look at it:

KINSALE WAR VICTIMS
RESENT GERMAN SEAMEN

No, you're wrong, this isn't going to be a tirade about
Irish hospitality or kicking a man when he's Downes or
anything like that ... at all. No, my point is that ... *there*
you have a perfect generic description of you Irish. After all,
what are ye BUT Kinsale war victims? What sort of a fight
did ye put up there, eh? And tell me this much – did yez
ever win a war? A *real* one? Fontenoy? Ah yes, I have read
about that particular day's work in the history books (of all
places). The Irish went out to Fontenoy, they chanced to
break up a charge by the English but were slaughtered to a
man. (Write no letters to the Editor about this statement –
I'm probably working from different history books ...). What
name do we today apply to this and a few cognate slaughters?
We call it 'the traditional ties between this country and
France'(!). No, the Irish never won a fight and I'll tell you
why. First, I grant that the Irishman is a good fighting man,
none better. The English is a good fighting man too, give him
a bit of cover and he'll fight till the cows come home. Do
you know the difference between the two? Well, here it is
now, once and for all – the English man is a married man and
that's why he'll do a good job, working away quietly, taking
good care of himself, blowing up the enemy – but not acting
the maniac, being 'brave' and running out and getting killed,

like Pat. See the difference *now*? The English man has responsibilities and won't act the fool; you crowd *will*! *You fellows aren't married men, that's why!* (Oh, I know, some of you have wives living in the house at home, but that's different, of course.)

What do you resent about the German seamen anyway? Do you think navies are immoral? Judging by the efforts you have made to establish one, I'd say you do.

The Dublin Man

There is a very rare creature called the king penguin. Advisedly I call it a creature because I do not know whether it is a fowl, a fish, or an animal: I am, however, in possession of the little-known fact that a spider is not an insect, but an animal.

Apparently changing the subject, I come to the statement so often made by Dublin statesmen that there is no foundation for the Belfast idea that there are two nations in Ireland and that therefore partition is justified. The two-nation idea is certainly false, but for this reason – that there are several nations in this country. You have, for example, a parcel of Cromwellian blackguards down south; they are called Yellabellies, otherwise Wexfordmen. Further south you have a settlement of iron-faced pigmies endowed with unearthly cuteness; these are called Kerrymen. Who could mistake a Galwayman for anything else? Indeed, I know certain Irish families which contain members of quite dissimilar nations, and all usually at war with one another. I hold, however, that Ireland's king penguin is the Dublin Man. I wish to attempt an analysis of this unique character and from time to time will endeavour to disclose to shrewder readers his more pronounced characteristics. These are embedded in the language he speaks, so that one may study him phrase by phrase. Today's phrase is

I WOULDN'T MIND ONLY.

Let us suppose you go into a pub. He is sitting behind a pint reading a newspaper. The pint is ignored – a portentous symptom.

Perhaps I should here digress to state this subtle concept in the abstract. The Dublin Man has no great objection to outrage on the part of other persons against himself. Immense outrage is accepted not so much with fortitude as with an air of weary disdain. He accepts tragedy as an unavoidable fundamental. What he will *under no circum-*

stances tolerate is a hostile gesture, however harmless, *that is gratuitous*. His intimate concern is with manners. Kill him – yes. That is to be expected. For all he knows you have a good reason. The instinct to kill is orderly and natural. He accepts it. But —— having killed him, *take the flint out of his petrol lighter . . .!!!!*

He is, let us say, the connoisseur of the unnecessary.

Let us now look at this attitude in its practical manifestation.

You find him in this mixture of gloom and lightning behind his pint. You are uncertain. You ask him: 'How is tricks?' and he says with what appears to be a smile that everything is game ball. Instantly divining that you are in the presence of the momentous, you talk about the weather; then – an uneasy pause. You wait. The next salute is this, said in an undertone, with dead-pan face.

'You heard, of course, that I was in digs?'

He well knows that you haven't heard no such a thing, and you dutifully tell him so.

'Ah, yes,' he says. 'In digs again after seventeen years of the happiest married life any man ever had. And I'll tell you what was a great consolation. The two of them was buried in the same grave.'

If you are yourself even one-eighth a true Dublin Man, your reaction will be instantaneous. You will say:

'Pairdin?'

A short pause here. Then:

'Ah, yes. The two is in the one grave.'

Observe the unique Dublin dual number in full flight.

'The two is in the one grave and I am back above in Heytesbury Street in digs with the young chisler Nicholas. You heard about the mad brother-in-law coming home on a visit out of the British Army three-quarters in the jigs?'

He asks you this question for the sole reason that he knows you never heard any such a thing.

'Ah yes. He come in one night with three bottles in him and a serviette out of the B. and I. dining room. I told Mary the wife to lave him alone. Give him his head, says I, and he'll be all right. Well in any case he began to fooster around the house and inside the hour he has the stairs on fire. I ordered all hands to the pumps, so to speak. We got the fire out after about an hour but in the meantime this character is inside the kitchen with all the taps in the gas meter full on, full bore. In any case the wife goes in and offers him a cigarette to get him out of the place and the next salute is the whole kitchen is blun up and the wife killed on the spot, without a scratch on your man. He then gets a hold of a sledge-hammer when I'm doing the needful about the wife and away up with him into an attic under the rafters. And I'll tell you one thing about this man. A decenter chiner never wore a hat. Bar he was jarred.'

'I see,' you then say, incredulously.

'Well in any case, when I got the wife's body covered under blankets, the brother-in-law was working on the ceiling with the sledge-hammer, working from above, and didn't the unfortunate poor man knock a lump of plaster down on Micky, the eldest boy. Killed him outright. After that our friend passes into some class of a coma. A hard case if you like. A character. I suppose I could call him my best friend. But a divil when he has the few jars on him. In any case I sent a message for the Guards and the doctors to come but at eight in the morning this character wakes up and says he is off for the day to go to Killarney on the Radio Express. How are you! There I was with the wife and the eldest dead, the half of the house in ruins – *and I wouldn't mind only on the way out he kicked the milk bottle to pieces and the young chisler Tomaus roaring his head off for his breakfast!*'

I trust the reader gets the point. Arson, murder, madness – these things are by the Dublin Man accepted with an indulgent smile. But the quite gratuitous fracture of a bottle of milk, extraneous to the anterior transaction, quite external to the former situation of drunkenness and passion . . . utterly unforgivable! Inexcusable lapse!

He then finishes the pint, folds the paper up until it is a cube of tiny dimension, smiles, and says: 'The good lady? I trust she is keeping well?' and out with him.

If you are a man – even a Kerryman – I hope you will be too astounded to reply to that one.

I will have more to say about the Dublin Man. Simple folk keep saying that Dublin is 'too big', the traffic is awful and rural Ireland is becoming depopulated. What nonsense! The sole function of rural Ireland is to provide the human ingredients for the constitution of the Dublin Man, who never lasts more than three generations in Dublin town. And I myself a Dublin Man? N.B.L!

*   *   *

It will be recalled that some weeks ago I undertook (too light-heartedly, alas) to disclose to readers the true nature of this character, the Dublin Man. Only when I came to close quarters was the immensity of the task manifest. I realise now that no human being of woman born – as in fact most are – can dissect or expound the Dublin Man. Have you ever met the Dublin Man who can claim a Dublin grandfather? Such does not exist. Rootless exracinate, the Dublin Man dies out and eternally is miraculously reborn. He is the unknowable fugitive, the incommunicate *maoufatan* of the Dublin streets. But dare not one attempt to present limited aspects of his character, granted that the ultimate *mystique* will be intact? Well, perhaps.

Once upon a time, in an immense inundation of vanity, I thought the Dublin Man might be analysed through his language. For example, minimum and chromium become *minium* and *chronyum*. A funeral is a *furenal*. There are many such words. Recently a Dublin Man (a 'newsboy' of sixtyone) told me that he had got drunk on 'wine' on a certain Sunday, and having nothing to do while the pubs were closed in the afternoon, appointed himself a car park attendant outside Croke Park, where a large match was in progress. 'When the crowd come out,' he said, 'I seen two priests come out. They come over to me and wan of them looks at me very hard. *Tell me, me good man*, says he, *do YOU take stilumants?*'

On another occasion, a Dublin Man who was doing some work for me inquired whether I had got the permission of the Corporation for certain alterations I had carried out inside a house. I told him I had not, that nobody would know about it, and enjoined him to keep his own mouth shut.

Sairtintly I will, he said, *but if they do find out, they'll be after you with a human cry.*

In my former article I tried to expound his usage of the

phrase *I wouldn't mind only* . . . He accepts unheard-of catastrophes and reverses with complacency. He makes no complaint. Why should he? Because – this was my theory – there
is bound to be on the part of his enemy some small breach of
etiquette, some trifling departure from decorum, which will
entitle the Dublin Man to let loose the full tidal wave of his
inner resentment and wrath. Go to his door and, when he
opens it, kick him in the stomach. That is quite all right
with him. But heaven help you if you bang his gate on your
way out. *I wouldn't mind oney he nearly destroyed me gate
going out.*

No, there is not much hope examining this character
through his speech. But here is something that arises from
observation: *the Dublin Man's attitudes to his wife and his
pint are identical.*

Summarise the situation thus:

He accepts both wife and pint as inevitable; he does not
like or dislike either; under no circumstances will he take
any notice whatever of either unless something extraordinary
happens (e.g. if either is knocked over in his presence). Both
are ordained companions, alternative, interchangeable,
similar, cognate even in contour. They are complementary.

The Dublin Man's technique is quite the same, whether
he is entering his bed chamber or a public house. He comes
in and stands near the counter. He is, of course, quite guilt-
less of the *gaffe* of ordering a pint. And let no simple reader
imagine he makes his needs known by gesture. He does
absolutely nothing at all that can be related to drinking. He
may fill his pipe or possibly scan a newspaper. But when a
soft, moist thud is heard, he carefully places eightpence on
the counter: he knows there is a pint there. He does not, of
course, see this pint. There must be, however, some mysterious method of cognition, some apparatus of invisible
pint antennae, to explain the phenomenon. Who has the
mind and the pen to convey to the stranger this grand and
portentous spectacle – the Dublin Man ignoring his pint!

And what is he at now? An old and dirty document is
produced from an inner pocket and minutely perused. It is
replaced. Very carefully the face of the clock is read. The
pipe is taken apart and prodded with wire.

Hey presto!

We have taken our eyes off them for one second and lo, both are gone! The Dublin Man *and* his pint have vanished. The tumbler stands, a veritable monument, with delicate traceries of foam slowly sinking to the bottom.

Trace, explain, unmask this Man? It can't be done. I tell you.

Sir Myles na Gopaleen's Family and Affairs

Myles Na gCopaleen is to accept an English title. The veteran Irish singer is to become a vassal of the British Crown, according to a story put out by A.P. from London last night. Considerable speculation has arisen in diplomatic circles here and across the Irish Sea as to the significance of the rumoured demarche on the part of a statesman whose relations with Western democratic governments have been so notoriously shaky throughout the course of the last three centuries. In Westminster the news has been received with considerable satisfaction and prominent political personages there do not conceal their view that the acceptance of the accolade will be in the nature of a triumph for old-fashioned British diplomacy. A military spokesman, in an inspired broadcast, referred to 'this distinguished old man whose services to the cause of humanity during the sombre crises of World Wars 1 and 2 can never be repaid . . .'; he added: '. . . His Majesty's Government are convinced that the man whom they have besought H.M. to decorate in so signal a manner is at once a great European and a great gentleman . . .' The attitude of the Irish papers, however, is, in general, restrained; the Government organs are cautious in tone and speak guardedly about the danger of mistaking eccentricity for genius, while several left-wing journals have criticised the former M.F.H. for what they regard as a betrayal of 'Celtic ideals'.

No details of the ceremony in which the honour will be conferred have so far been forthcoming, but it is understood on good authority that all formality will most probably be dispensed with, as the brave old gentleman who is to be the central figure is now confined, by infirmity, to a wash-hand-basin-chair. Meanwhile serious rioting has again broken out in Dublin and clashes between armoured cars and terrorists from the Myles na gCopaleen Monarchist Clubs have been reported from several suburbs. A number of battalions of the military have been drafted in to deal with the disturbances and curfew has been proclaimed in the city area. Another report says that members of the Myles na gCopaleen 'Gold Shirts', a small group of plutocratic terrorists, last night came to blows with 'Fenians', be-caubed thugs from the Cruiskeen Lawn Clubs on the North Quays, outside a café in O'Connell Street. Tables and chairs were used as weapons, and also some food, and five civilians and five soldiers were injured, in addition to three hundred reported dead or missing, before military police arrived on the scene and attempted to restore order. On Tuesday the Government buildings were evacuated eighteen times as a result of messages broadcast from 'Radio Eireann', the illegal secret radio, warning officials that the buildings were mined.

Feeling also runs high in the mountain country where Mr James Dillon, a well-known Irish politician, in a spirited speech to constituents, accused the Government of cowardice and foolishness and stated that they had made a great mistake in alienating Myles na gCopaleen by their persistently unfriendly attitude to a man who, he must insist, was undoubtedly the best man in Ireland and his own sworn friend. 'Nevertheless,' he added, 'we cannot shut our eyes to the fact that a dark cloud is overshadowing us. Irish Ireland is stunned and shocked by a gross and wicked betrayal on the part of their whilom champion and erstwhile friend. It is a conspiracy prearranged in Paris; I cannot understand how Myles na gCopaleen has committed in cold blood a breach of faith.'

An attempt to reach settlement was made late last night in Dublin when representatives of the 'Gold Shirts' and the 'Fenians' met at a round table conference under the auspices of the Department of Industry and Commerce, which has just returned to Dublin for a few months from Washington. Ways and means were discussed and solutions suggested but the conference ultimately exploded in the noisiest uproar yet echoed by the walls of the Kildare Street building over the Gold Shirts' demand that the matter should be submitted to the arbitration of an adjudicator from London, a Mr Dermot McMurrough. Utter pandemonium broke

loose when Mr Molotov, rising on a point of order, launched
a direct attack on Myles na gCopaleen accusing him of 'thin-
veiled murder' and the burning of the Reichstag. Mr Oliver
Flanagan asked if it were not a fact that Myles na gCopaleen
had for the last twenty-five years been an accredited British
spy, who also drew large sums of gold from a source in
Moscow? More than four hundred of the delegates rose at
this point shouting 'Order' and were removed by secret
military police. Later, when order had been restored, Myles
na gCopaleen sat glumly in the dock while the chief prose-
cutor had this to say about his political record: 'Myles na
gCopaleen's claim to have fought in the G.P.O. in '16 is a
lie, a cynical, blasphemous lie, uttered by a man whose
conscience did not hesitate before murder, and whose
honour did not prevent him from committing perjury. He
does not deserve to be refuted, for the facts established by us
are irrefutable . . .'

Interviewed at his house in Santry after the trial Myles
na gCopaleen said that he was deeply touched by the British
Government's offer. He had no information about the
ceremony but assumed that something informal was en-
visaged. 'I hope to meet His Majesty at Kingstown and
proceed from thence to the Mansion House for the main
ceremony, which will be quite simple,' he said, adding,
roguishly, 'Mr Reynolds will be my train-bearer!' Asked
what title he would assume Myles na gCopaleen showed
surprise and inquired of interviewers what title they thought
he should assume. 'Lord Bacon' was suggested, and also
'Marshal Law'. Myles na gCopaleen smiled and said: 'I
thought you knew! The fact is, gentlemen, I am henceforth,
by letters patent, to be . . . Mr na gCopaleen . . .'

* * *

The paralysis of Irish industrial and literary life as a result
of the strike at Cruiskeen Industries (Eire), Ltd, has not,
happily, quite halted the eternal vigilance which the Sage of
Santry has pronounced to be the price of freedom. Scab
or no scab, a secret lodge has been constituted to look after
major national issues, and if necessary, in time of emergency,
to take over the Administration. The Cruiskeen Courier
Service is now in full operation (it was blueprinted in nine-

teen and forty-four when David Gray threatened to declare war on the Irish Nation) and nothing escapes the Unsleeping Eye. You talk about the empire upon which the sun never sets? You don't know the half of it.

Once it is known or suspected that vigilance is relaxed, there is a tendency to lawlessness. One can do very little about this situation. Whoever is responsible for the human face has a lot to answer for in this regard.

Very good. Let us now to our muttons.

Two fellows got out of line yesterday morning. Which of them got out of line first I do not know. Adjudication on that particular issue will ultimately rest in the more than capable hands of Fred Mangan, or maybe Walter Molony. Eventually Tadhg Forbes will be dragged into it, and *that* means only wan thing – we are going to appeal. At the heel of the hunt we will find ourselves confronted by Judge Mac-Carthy, whose decision we will undher no saircumstances accept, and our last situation – the identity of this 'we' is immaterial – will be as good as our first, we will find ourselves up in front of Conor Maguire himself.

Before I forget what I am supposed to be talking about, I must bring you back to the junction of Holles Street and Merrion Square. (I was about to qualify the latter street title by adding 'East' or 'West' or some such word until I realised that there was, after all, only one Holles Street.) (And one is enough, from what I see going on.) In any case – see picture – a motor car, and a C.I.E. bus were in a sort of collision. The transaction was arranged apparently on the basis that 'Cruiskeen Lawn' was on strike and that any gesture, however extravagant, would get by.

(Observe, all ye who toy with Communism, how what appear to be very firmly established organs of public order collapse at the whisper of trouble in high places. The rats of human society are ever on the watch. Give them half a chance and you've had it!)

To digress momentarily——

Peaceable citizens who live in Dublin are obsessed by the ubiquity of policemen. They are stuck in doorways, under trees, in the more rural parts. In central Dublin they spend their time taking down the number of parked cars, and in one way or another intimidating every manner of taxpayer.

Observe, however, that our police force in Dublin, who have arranged our traffic on the basis that a carefully planned mess is better than a casual mess are very scientific lads. The squad cars, wherein ride the *élite* of the rozzers, have gigantic aerials, wireless valves, the divilanall machinery inside the bonnet to apprehend criminals. Not the penalty, but the certainty of swift and sure detection, deters the law-breaker. Right. The traffic incident pictured above occurred at 10.55 a.m. Instantly both parties concerned rushed for the telephone, housed in an asbestos shed hard by, dialling the magic '999', which is what you ring when a burglar has his fingers round your neck throttling you (to death).

I certify that the police car arrived on the scene to investigate at midday precisely, or sixty-five minutes after the accident. The distance between the accident and the nearest three or four police stations is about half a mile.

In the meantime both vehicles were locked in the centre of the highway, causing an obstruction, as well as a serious hazard, to passing traffic.

The police car contained two officers. One was in uniform; the other in flannel pants and miscellaneous summer attire.

To Kinnane, revered Dublin police boss, I address the following pithy words of good advice:

1 When an accident obstructing the highway happens in central Dublin, arrange that your men will get there within an hour, even if they have to use bath-chairs.

2 Tell your boys – from me – to dress themselves.

* * *

Funny thing, if you walked into the (inner sanctum) of the Director of the Myles na gCopaleen Banking Corporation, you would find on the (massive) telephone-burdened desk a strange and rather coarse-looking confection – grey ghastly gnarled pastry bulging out of a large high-walled dish as if inflated with some deadly gas. This is (none other than) (our old friend) humble pie. Employees of the Corporation who steal 'money' or make a mess of their figures are (hauled) in before the Director and made to eat some of the pie.

That is nothing, of course. I am supreme Governor of the

bank and in my own (palatial) office, you'll find an enormous trough filled with dirt. This is the dirt the Director himself has to eat when I ring for him and demand to know why he discounted our non-fiduciary coupons without first ensuring 'parity' of 'drain' by increasing marginally our holding of immature fee-warrants.

* * *

A lightning strike has taken place among the employees of Cruiskeen Industries, Ltd, a subsidiary of the Cruiskeen Corporation. Cruiskeen Industries, Ltd, produce 'Cruiskeen Lawn' for the *Irish Times*.

The *Irish Times* Editorial Board, in a message issued last night, states:

It is regretted that, owing to lightning strike action taken by two employees of Cruiskeen Industries, Ltd, (Eire), the customary edition of 'Cruiskeen Lawn' does not appear today. This arises from circumstances entirely outside the Board's control.

The facts of the situation are as follows. Two 'ghosts' (second class) who are employed to comb provincial papers to find and write up evidence damaging to the G.A.A. demanded £50 per week 'danger money', stating that they had received several threats, including one from a member of the Faughs team that he would 'lam' them. They were informed that this claim should be presented in the normal manner through the Cruiskeen Conciliation Council, who were empowered to refer it, in default of agreement, to the Labour Court. The two officers failed to report for file duty on Saturday night, and were formally suspended by the Foreman Night Ghost. A picket was put on the *Irish Times* premises at 1.10 a.m. on Sunday morning. Members of the Cruiskeen Latin Bureau, who were due for duty at 3 a.m., refused to pass the picket. It was learnt later that the members of the Steam and Traction Branch had come out in sympathy with the strikers and it is expected that by this morning all Bureaus and Branches will be affected including K. & C., Social Comment, Pun and Cliché, Gaelic Literature, Deutschwissenschaft, Drama, Cod Detection, Denunciation and Abuse, as well as various sub-offices and country lodges. It is understood that the strike, which is unofficial, will not be sanctioned by the two unions to which the men belong – the Irish Transport and General Workers' Union and the Stationary Engine Drivers' and Boilermakers' Union. It is understood a strike committee has been formed. The Board has intimated that it will not negotiate until the men have returned to work. It expresses to the public its regret for this occurrence, which arises from no fault of the Board.

A correspondent writes:

The news that the Cruiskeen organisation is yet another national undertaking to be paralysed over-night by the weapon of the unofficial lightning strike will come as a shock even to a nation already almost resigned to the hardships caused by this irresponsible method of agitation. It is understood that there is already on hand a small quantity of raw, unrefined Cruiskeen which is being processed by an emergency scab staff recruited from the *Standard* newspaper; but when this is exhausted, there will be no Cruiskeen in the country for an indefinite period. There is a possibility that remaining stocks will be rationed so as to cause the minimum hardship to those most closely affected. There is no prospect of importing supplies, as the product is not made outside the country. The strike committee have refused a permit for the production of limited supplies of new Cruiskeen for use in hospitals and in old people's homes. It is regarded as fortunate that this deplorable occurrence has coincided with warm weather, as the effect on persons confined indoors by hard weather would precipitate a serious crisis.

In Cabinet circles there is deep concern at the possibility of a protracted period of time within which national affairs will not be adequately dealt with and placed in proper perspective, but suitable measures are already blue-printed to deal with public disorder or undue unrest. Military and police leave has been cancelled.

Even if the strike were settled immediately, it would take several days to re-start the organisation: the strike committee have refused a request to allow a skeleton staff for maintenance work and to prevent the rebukes, replies, ripostes, rejoiners and retorts from cooling.

Comment from the Boilermakers' Union:

'We have only this morning received a memorandum from the strike committee enumerating the grievances of the men and until this document has been studied no comment will be possible.'

A member of the strike committee interviewed stated that this strike would never be settled. There was no question of negotiations. The two ghosts had been treated with an unheard-of manifestation of truculence and contemptuous invidiousness coupled with unprecedented disrespect for the fundamental rights of all mankind the like of which did not exist even among the besotted barbarian communities inhabiting mountainous lands and obscure tundra east of the notorious Iron Curtain. No unbridled exhibition of force or unparalleled display of anarchical lust for capitalist vengeance against the two defenceless ghosts would intimidate the strike committee or abate by one iota their iron resolve to march steadfastly ahead in closed phalanx shoulder to shoulder in defence of the immutable and transcendentally indefeasible and ineluctable principle of a coherent and inter-locking democratic *bloc*, irrevocably dedicated to the realisation in a practical and decent society of the concept of the duty of all who esteem democratic principles to band together, one with the other, in an ultimate, convulsive and final battle against the unutterable depravities and excesses of the cynical and sordid capitalistic octopus, the Chairman, otherwise known as the Beast of Santry.

A reporter who telephoned the house in Santry was told that 'the master is in bed. He has been arranging for the foundation of a mammoth new Irish film industry and had dinner here tonight in the Great Hall with Sir Alexander Korda and his brother Sir Sum. He is not to be disturbed.'

* * *

Meine erste Bekanntschaft mit Myles na gCopaleen machte ich in der *Irish Times* im Jahre 1940, namentlich, als er 'Cruiskeen Lawn' begann. Mein erster Eindruck, der sich bald immer mehr vertiefte, war, dass Myles ein Neu-Irisch schreibt, das geschmackvoll, hoeflich und wissen-schaftlich ist.

Ein Laken mit einigen Nadeln oder Nadelstichen so zu befestigen, dass es die Bloessen deckt, kann jeder ohne zu lernen: aber ein Rock machen, in dem wir Sonntags in die Kirche gehen, kann er nicht machen ohne zu lernen und zu ueben. Gute Schneider fallen nicht vom Himmel, und Leute, die *von selbst* ihre Muttersprache als litterarische Sprache schreiben koennen, auch nicht. Viel Neuirisch——

SLANABHAILE: Kawd ay so ataw er shool agut inenima-teerna?

MISE: *Sliocht as litir chineálta atá faghálta agam ón dochtúir Otto Beideseiten.*

SLANABHAILE: Ogus kay ay fayn?

MISE: *Ollamh ollscoile i Zurich ins an Eilbhéis. Tá sé ar an ollscoil san mar* Professor fuer Sanskrit und Vergleichende Sprachwissenschaft.

SLANABHAILE: Ogus kawd taw á raw igeh?

MISE: *Eist go gcluinfidh tú*. Viel Neuirisch, das in den letzten 35 Jahren gedruckt worden ist, faellt mehr oder weniger unter die eben gegebene Charakteristik: es ist dunkel und schwer verstaendlich, nicht weil die irische Sprache unbeholfen oder dunkel waere, oder weil die zum Ausdruck kommenden Gedanken tief und unergruendlich waeren, sondern weil die betreffenden Schriftsteller nicht gelernt haben, einfache Dinge auch einfach und natuerlich *schriftlich* auszudruecken. 'Ne sutor supra crepidam!' moechte man oft ausrufen.

SLANABHAILE: Inenimday! Govóradeea urinn!!

MISE: Zwischen diesen beiden Sorten von Neu-Irisch haelt Myles na gCopaleen, wie zwischen Scylla und Charybdis, die gute Mitte. Sein Irisch is wissenschaftlich aber auch bodenstaendig——

SLANABHAILE: Naw vwilir kreekniheh fós?

MISE: *Táim, go raibh maith agat.*

SLANABHAILE: Ogus kad ay an changa ee sunn? Graygish?

MISE: *Ní headh. Laidean.*

SLANABHAILE: Tigim. Guramahagut.

* * *

History was again made at Rineanna yesterday when an enormous green-painted Skymaster touched down after making the Atlantic crossing in the record time of three hours two minutes. The plane was the *Cruiskeen,* flagship of Hiberno-American Air-Lions Incorporated, gigantic international menagerie operators, who were making their first survey flight. On board, in addition to the crew and five passengers, were Sir Myles na gCopaleen (the da), President of the Corporation, his two cousins Sir Sitric and Sir Hosis na gCopaleen, Directors, all attired in teddy-bear coats, and smoking cigars. The gentlemen were warmly welcomed by the airport officials, and were subsequently entertained to lunch by the Department of Industry and Commerce. In the evening the party travelled to Ennis where they were the guests of honour at a banquet given by the Ennis Chamber of Commerce.

'Make no mistake about it,' Sir Myles told a reporter, 'our interest lies right here in Rineanna. You got the right idea here, the right Government, and Rineanna is in the right place. Americans are mighty proud about Rineanna. Only your Government got ideas, where was your contract for refuelling American planes? Rineanna's fine. It'll be better when you have put down real runways. We like them longer – maybe ten miles.'

Asked whether he thought that the development of air-craft with ever-lengthening range would result in the ultimate bypassing of Rineanna, Sir Myles said: 'Not a chance. Make no mistake about it, Rineanna's a big thing. Our interest's right here. Bigger runways and your airport is a peach. Rineanna's no mushroom junk. Maybe every place is by-passed some time. But Rineanna's here for a long time.'

Asked how long, Sir Myles referred to the essentially slow nature of aeronautic research, stressing the difficulty of designing large planes with economic payload. 'You won't see the big babies for a long time. Maybe weeks, maybe months. Look how long Foynes lasted. My company's very proud about Rineanna. This business of flying lions and animals is big stuff, and Eire's in, right on the ground floor. When we get the sixty-engined Cloud Liners, we aim to fly elephants. The cousin Sir Hosis is organising far ahead. Shipping big animals doesn't pay. We've worked it out and we know.'

The Skymaster left later for Hurn, leaving behind Sir Hosis, who was detained at Ennis on business. It is under-stood that the name of the company, Hiberno-American Air-Lions Incorporated, is shortly to be changed to Pan-Am-Eire-aan Hareways.

Among the five passengers landed was Miss Minnie Glaubenspiegel, who is of Irish extraction and whose parents hail from Pettigo. She told a reporter that though she had never been in Ireland before, she had no sense of strangeness and found the Irish people courteous, witty and charming. She hoped to spend at least two days in Pettigo before flying on to rejoin her husband whose home is in Vilna. 'Perhaps,' she said with a smile, 'I may come back one day. Who knows?'

Among the passengers was also Julius S. Dreckdurch-suchen, President of the St Patrick's Guild of Irish-American Brotherhood, who is half-Irish and has relatives living in Borris-in-Ossory. Before flying on to Hurn, he told a reporter: 'I aim to be back here before Christmas. You can tell your paper that we Americans look with great respect on Irish talent, we venerate Ireland as a very old nation. Your writers have a big reputation in the States, but a lot of them got the wrong publishers. We Irish should get together and stick together. I aim to export your whiskey, your tweeds, and I'm dead set on getting the right sort of contacts for your writers in the States. When I get back I want to meet *everybody* in Ireland. I want to look everything over and then I reckon we're going to do business. Don't let neutrality in the war bother you. America was neutral too remember.'

Another Skymaster is expected today.

From Day to Day

Continuing my reminiscences on the early issues of Cruiskeen Lawn (which were mostly in Irish), several correspondents accused this newspaper of 'spewing' on Irish and seeking to make the language ridiculous by publishing puns in it. One day it appeared in English, and another man wrote:

Today we have the Cruiskeen in unadorned English. Read it to the office boy or to any of your friends at tea on Sunday evening and ask them if they think it's funny – or even humorous. And this is the genius you have imported into the *Times* to debunk the ridiculosities of Gaelic enthusiasts! . . . Doing the 'gawm' for public amusement is a bit out of date – even in Irish.

Then the Gaelic Literary Society of U.C.D. passed a formal resolution of congratulation. I did not know of this to-do at the time, as I was then living in Monaco (in tirement), so I kept cheerfully on.

Funny time we lived in then!

Funny? Yerrah, I don't know. An odd thing happened at this time. I began to write a little book called the *Béal Bocht*. It was – all right, it was a wee bit satirical. In fact, it was a ferocious and highly technical onslaught on the Gaels; I was at the same time busily learning English.

While this book was in course of composition – a mere month or so – the news leaked out and a famous firm of Dublin publishers asked me whether it would be possible for them to be permitted the privilege of publishing it. Why be shy nowadays about the name of the firm? It was the good house of Browne and Nolan. A little flattered by this forwarding-seeing, this spirit of native enterprise, I said: *Certainly, ye shall have the manuscript as soon as it's ready.*

Well, the book came out in due course, and sold twelve thousand copies. Your Irish 'novelists' who 'write' in English think they are very successful men if they sell two thousand copies of their stuff, and only the other day we had this Club Leabhar crowd boasting that it might be possible to sell as many as two thousand copies of a Gaelic work! God bless my soul, I done it all ten years ago.

But the *Béal Bocht* was not published by Browne and Nolan's. For why? Because the report of their reader on the great book was in the following terms:

I can safely assert that in an experience of sixty years this is quite the craziest piece of Irish I have ever met.

What most surprises me is the self-assurance of its author – a man who demonstrates twenty times on every page that he is the veriest tyro in the Irish language. For want of knowledge he cannot begin, or continue or finish a sentence properly. Constructions such as he writes have never before been seen in Irish, and one earnestly hopes that nothing of the kind will ever be repeated.

The late Stephen McKenna at one time proposed to write a book

How to Write Irish
by
One Who Can't

and here, I am convinced, we have an author who could take up his project with every hope of success.

Chapter II of the typescript is devoted, almost entirely, to a description of a sickly and stinking pig whose odoriferousness was such as to cause a horse to turn back, and to drive a certain family into exile! The author may reply that the whole thing is an extravaganza, but if every word of his text were a *genuine* pearl, jem or jewel, the inferiority of the Irish would damn the production.

At first I put a pencil mark against every solecism of his, but the marks became so numerous that I was obliged to give up the idea, and to erase those I had made.

My advice to you is —— to spend none of the firm's money on this work.

That is absolute gospel. Even the word 'jem' is exact.

Mr Frank Aiken had something to say the other day about the merits of commercial publication as distinct from publication by a State concern. Let him ponder the foregoing and think again on what faces the young Gaelic author.

*   *   *

I have been studying the characteristics and habits of civil servants for years because they are in reality very interesting persons. (Persons, mind – not people.) The public's conception of the civil servant is usually at Varian's with the facts. (Varian's can even put new bristles on old facts!) Let's take a look at the day of a typical Higher Ex-Active Officer, Acting, Unestablished, Grade IV, proceeding on the scale £180-5-190, with cost of living malus and Children's Hollow Ounces.

Observe that he does not go into his office in the morning. He proceeds from his residence towards his office. When he reaches his office, even then he does not go into it – forbears even to enter it. He attends at his office. By means of this ingenious tactic he is now *in* his office.

There are large mounds of documents on his desk. These represent his 'work'. He frowns slightly. He views his work with grave concern. Certain portions of it he views with anxiety. In his view, there is pressure of work. The work is, however, under consideration. Certain separate matters are under review, others are under active consideration. A decision will be taken only on consideration of the facts in all their aspects. These facts will, in the meantime, be under continuous and active review and a decision will be announced at an early date. At the moment he finds himself unable to concur in any suggestion that any of these matters, at that moment, fall to be dealt with by him.

He seats himself and opens the *Irish Times* in order to ascertain whether his department has been attacked again. He does this by reading the concluding sentence of the leading article. 'Is it too much to hope that even at this late hour these cumbrous interdependent and interlocking statutes will be replaced by a comprehensive measure that is related to the exigent needs of the present day?' It *has* been attacked again. He smiles; then attends to official business, transacting it.

At 1 p.m. he relinquishes duty and (actually) goes home for lunch. At 2.30 p.m. he is again engaged on having matters under active consideration in all their aspects. He requests the early submission of further details. At 5.30 p.m. he relinquishes duty. Travels home in a large public service vehicle. He consumes edible dishes prepared by his wife. He takes light exercise in his garden. At 11.30 p.m. he opts out of his clothes and retires.

*   *   *

About four years ago I was reading, at 3 a.m., a thing called
'M. TVLLII CICERONIS . . . AD T. POMPONIVM ATTICVM.'

These documents purport to be the correspondence
between Cicero and Atticus, at a moment of the former's
decline. I was astounded by one paragraph in the earlier
letters. This paragraph mentioned something quite unknown
to the preChristian Romans. This led me to the idea that the
Cicero letters are a fake, and one of the glories of what Con
Curran calls the renascence. Fair enough, I'm only an Irishman. The point appears to be that if I can *prove*, as distinct
from asserting, that these 'historic' documents are fakes, a
certain number of faces will be red. More particularly, that
of a certain recent British scholar.

At the same time, the immutable is the immutable.
Dubalin is still Dublin. Our peculiar destiny is that we live
here. The fact appears to be that Republic of Ireland gets
along with Jack Nugent or else. It's just like that.

A VOICE: I suppose that'a crack against Jack Costello. I
take a very poor view about that coming from yerself that
I always thought was a dacent unfortunate, and I seen me
own mother goin' down with the potata skins in the olden
days to find the sticks of fur-nitature out on the street just
because the rates wasn't ped.

MYSELF (*very sternly*): It's Jack Nugent of the Dolphin
I'm talking about, not Costello. I am only trying to get an
anecdote out of me before it strangles me.

I went into the Dolphin the other evening, embracing
a vellum-bound copy of Cicero's 'letters', roared for a
'dozen' (oysters, Oi need hardly say!), did a bit of further
reading, and then turned, very excited, white-faced to a
congregation of bookies eating stake in my company. (Very
much *stet* as regards 'stake'!)

'Listen, lads,' I roared, 'those letters of Cicero is all a
fake, I can prove it.'

Nothing at all happened for a few minits.

I then heard a rather low-pitched dragging roar. It was
caused by the face of a customer being disengaged from the
cauliflower. He come up to me, wiping himself around the face
and neck, and carefully going with his napkin inside the
faultless white collar he thought he had on but in fact hadn't.

'Say that again,' he said.

'Sairtintly,' I responded.

And I did so. I explained that the alleged letters from Cicero to Atticus contained references – some of which I enumerated – which proved that the letters were phoneys, that they must have been written in the Middle Ages by idle monks with a taste for mischief and, generally speaking, that the whole job was all my eye and Betty Martin.

'What did you say his name was again?' my companion asked.

At this juncture the manager of the Dolphin, Greeley, came up, and asked was everything all right.

'Sairtintly everything's all right,' says I.

My companion glared at Greeley and said to me, in the loudest stage whisper possible:

'Could I see you alone for a moment?'

'Sairtintly,' I said.

We then walked the statutory four paces away from everybody.

'Say that name again,' he said, somewhat menacingly.

'Cicero,' I said.

'You don't mean to tell me,' he said, 'that you're in the hands of that fellow?'

Here I made a gesture of abasement, cursing myself for mixing up horses and books. (The 'books' rarely make the same error!)

'Because I'm going to tell you this much,' says this character. 'I'm not going to have it. You're a friend of mine and so far as I know you're supposed to be a relation of mine as well, because the married sister is supposed to be a cousin of the first wife that's dead now. R.I.P. What was the name again?'

'Cicero.'

'He got a dog stopped the other night.'

'Is that so?'

'A greater hook never stud in shoe-leather.'

'And he stopped the best two-yur-old about a week ago. Don't I know him well? Didn't he touch me for a fiver?'

'A curious formula for friendship and acquaintance,' I remarked. 'Fivers.'

This other fellow then gazes carefully into a nearby fire.
Then he says, meticulously:

'I suppose I needn't tell you about that crowd?'

I observe him. He means every word he says. I await the
superbly temporarising and banal remark which duly comes.

'Do you know what I mean?' he says.

'I think I do,' I say, solicitously.

(He then becomes overtly morose, gazes steadily at the
toes of the varnished shoes and says, quite casually:)

'But shure all that crowd is mad.'

Where reader, in this fabulous context, do you lave the
present Excellency with his slim volume of Latin prose?

Where do you think I really *ought* to be?

In heaven, of course.

(If the ciners would have me!)

*   *   *

British insurance companies, parasitic organisations whose
tentacles extend to this country, immobilising and sterilising
our scanty capital, are becoming more and more scared of
being 'nationalised' or 'mutualised' by the present régime
in Britain. One line of defence they have adopted is the
publication of expensive and quite hysterical advertisements,
to be compared – if one looks for an analogy here – with an
'apology' recently tendered to the public by the butchers and
promising that henceforth only low-grade meat would be
retailed by them. Consider the following fairy tale published
in a London paper and 'issued by the Industrial Life
Officers':

Among the policyholders I call on regularly is a nice little
woman in Leopold Road. She held a policy on her father's life
and paid the premiums like clockwork. Then, quite suddenly she
disappeared. Instead of her cheerful smile and a cup of tea in the
kitchen I found a bolted door with the paper under the knocker
and the milk still on the doorstep.

Her neighbour wasn't much help. She'd seen her go off the
afternoon before. No, she'd left no message except to say that her
father was ill.

Next week it was the same. No answer to my knock except a
hollow echo in the hall. No further news from the neighbours. So
it went on, until I even gave up going through the gate. I could
see by the state of her step she wasn't back.

By this time I was getting worried because her unpaid premiums were piling up. So I decided to ask my Head Office to help.

Head Office soon got busy. Some days later they notified me that the missing woman had been traced to her father's home in Bradford. He had been taken suddenly and seriously ill and she had left at a moment's notice to nurse him. Our local agent had contacted her and had collected the unpaid premiums, which in her anxiety she had entirely overlooked.

A month later back at Leopold Road, she told me her father had just died and said how much she appreciated the trouble we had taken to find her so that the policy on her father's life was fully maintained.

I tell you, the gratitude on that woman's face when I settled her claim made me feel proud to be part of an organisation which has contributed so much to human happiness and security. Her story is just one example of how we spare no pains to protect the interests of our policyholders.

Did you ever in your life hear the like?

The facts are as follows. I know what I am talking about for a change. Researchers in the *Irish Times* Enniscorthy bureau have checked up. Person in question is Mrs Gawskawn, wife of local razor-blade salesman, keen reader of *People* newspaper. Here is what happened:

One morning a swarthy masher drove up to the door in a Riley car, knocked, and asked Mrs Gawskawn whether she wanted the blades of her lawn mower sharpened. Mrs Gawskawn courteously declined, noting, however, the engaging trim of the audacious stranger's moustache. The latter gallantly said that he was not accustomed to take No for an answer.

'Perhaps,' he added archly, 'we might talk the problem over. Your husband . . .?'

'He is selling razor blades in Cork.'

'A pity. However, I think we had better thrash this thing out over a steak below in Jack MacCarthy's hotel in the Glen of the Downs, otherwise it might lead to a frustrative imbalance which might well lead to a permanent psychosis.'

The crossroads! What was a small girl of forty-seven, ignorant of the ways of the world, the world of men, to decide? The insurance man was due in two hours? Her husband would make his scheduled phone call at ten

demanding to know whether her father was yet dead. Yet
withal, what had she got from life? Years of child-bearing
had impaired her figure – true. But had she utterly lost that
magic, that unutterable something which had snared the
man who was ultimately to lead her to the altar? (Actually,
it had been her father who had led her, the present wall-
faced husband with his six pounds five a week having skulked
in by a side-door at the last minute, when the so-called
ceremony was more or less over, so to speak.) No! Life still
offered its timeless challenge. Here was a handsome gentleman offering to sharpen the blades of her lawn mower,
having arrived in a Riley car, probably a demonstration
model sold £200 off the list price. An impostor obviously, a
sort of Scarlet Pimpernel, a Baron Münchhausen for all *she*
knew.

'Perhaps you would step this way while I get my things,'
she said.

Too late to go back. There is no use walking out on life.
The insurance man? Bah!

'I simply cannot define it,' said Ronald, 'but . . . your
eyes! They are so deep and secret. Your lips for me amount
to the sum of all temptations. I want you to come with me
to the roof of the hotel and look out through this telescope.'

Yes, it was true. One could almost hear the pipes of elf-
land faintly blowing. Down near Rathcoole, sitting on the
sea with the graceful disdain of a swan, was a four-engined
Labrador Hawk.

'Darling,' he said huskily, 'we have had a good lunch from
Jack. You must have dinner with me . . . in the Bahamas . . .
at Butlin's.'

'Sweetness . . .!' No other words could be summoned to
the coral lips and soon the couple, who by now loved each
other dearly were heading for the foreign clime at alt. 4,500
approx.

Time, as is its wont, passed.

'Suppose the bottom were to fall out of razor blades,' he
had said one evening through the lazy curl of his after-
dinner cigar, 'what then?'

'I dare not think of such matters,' she had riposted sadly.

'You must face life,' he had said fiercely. 'Yourself and

your unfortunate husband will be on the rates, and after
that you will be on the side of the road if the County Manager
doesn't like you. Let's get married, sweet. Forget the past.'

Again . . . the crossroads! Only a master artist, fitted to
probe the secrets of a woman's heart, could attempt to
delineate the tempest that then raged in the breast of Mrs
Gawskawn. Would she give up this man, deny herself forever the charming conversation he was wont to dispense, for
aye? Or follow Love's beckon, the summons of Cupid,
knowing that what is natural must be good? But . . . *the
insurance man*? By now he would have come and gone. And
the other Man in her Life? 'I'll put you down for two gross
five-blade packets,' he would now be saying, 'and two gross
ten-blade and I'm glad it's the end of the week. Always glad
to get home to the little woman.'

'It can never be, Ronald,' she said, averting her gaze into
the fat palms. 'You see, I am a Protestant.'

'But darling . . .'

'Do not look at me, do not touch me. Promise me, Ronnie.
I am going to walk out of your life, Ronnie, darling, our love is
too fierce. It must not be. I am going, Ronnie. Always I will
think of you. I am going, Ronnie. Oh, Ronnie, I'm gone . . .'

'Darling . . .'

And homeward by giant Skymaster, few suspecting the
turbulence a lone woman can carry in her mother's heart.
Suppose, though, the insurance man got tired calling, would
never call again ever? Impossible! Ridiculous!

Yes – he's at the gate, same old curly-headed six pounds
five a week. She flies to his arms.

'My pet,' he mutters huskily. 'I'm so glad you're back.
And I have great news for you. Your old man died yesterday
and . . . close your eyes . . . I have a surprise. There is somebody in the drawn room waiting to see you . . .'

'Not *the insurance man*?'

'Yes . . . with a little (*coyly*) . . . a little . . . cheque!'

'O darling, I am so happy.'

* * *

I have taken note of some observations on the lately con-
cluded war of liberation made by Mr Kingsmill Moore in the

columns of the *Irish Daily Times* last Friday – reckoning by
your terrestrial time – and since some of these observations
might lead some of my students into grave error *de veritatis
natura, de animae salute* and indeed, worst of all, *de me*, I am
constrained to speak out today without Fuehrer favour. One
or two points only will I have time to deal with and the first
must be the opening sentence of the document with the
uttering of which the defendant is charged. 'Let us try to get
this thing right and in perspective,' it says. That, of course,
is a wholly inadmissible exordium and may not hereinafter
be used. It means 'I desire to put before the public some
eccentric and personal views, pretending that they must be
the views of all reasonable people'; or 'I desire, in the guise
of stating certain objective and unexceptionable propositions,
to let off some steam'.

Obedience to the laws of the State and conformity in action to
its foreign policy is not only a civil duty, it is usually a moral
duty. But it may come into conflict with what the citizen conceives to be a greater moral duty . . .

That is an extract from the impounded document. There
is, let it be said at once, to theologians approved by me no
such thing known as a civil duty. Every duty of whatsoever
kind is a moral duty, though for convenience of exposition it
is permissible to divide the corpus of moral duties into
categories, as family duties, religious duties, duties related
to the diffusion of unsavoury literature, chrematistic duties,
etc., etc. When therefore I hear someone say that one moral
duty may come into conflict with what the citizen conceives
to be a greater moral duty, in charity I conclude that I have
not heard aright. Giving a man all my substance, on the one
hand, and murdering him on the other, cannot both be
moral duties, nor is conflict possible in any matter affecting
truth and morals.

'It was wrong,' the document says elsewhere, 'to throw
stones through the windows of those who were legitimately
rejoicing. But which of us when a student has not done
wrong and foolish things . . .?'

In the first place it is usually wrong to throw stones
through other people's windows at all and their rejoicing –

and the legitimacy thereof – has no bearing whatever on the matter. Almost unlimited comment is possible on that question at the end. (The answer to it? Myself, of course.) If the entire herd of humans is to be embraced in the phrase 'which of us', will it not be a bit puzzling to the window-breaking chislers of Gardner Street, who were never, so far as they can recall, students in the sense of being well-dressed little rowdies? Most amazing of all is the implication that each one of 'us' did wrong and foolish things 'when a student'. Pray . . . does nobody . . . at all . . . *ever* . . . do wrong and foolish things when no longer a student? Were the architects of your late war *all* students?

As an Irishman who all his life has endeavoured to promote understanding and good relations between Ireland and England . . . may I appeal that those incidents should be forgotten . . .?

I hold that no person of the age of, say, five, could undertake any effective inter-racial pacifications. I say – acidly – that 'understanding' and 'good relations' in that context are antonyms, mutually irreconcilable. Paudrig Crohoore and J. Bull, on the most superficial of acquaintanceships, simply do not fancy each other; get them to understand each other better and their distaste will deepen. And by whom should these incidents be forgotten? Myself? Am I then no longer permitted to remember Limerick?

Frankly, I think the promotion of these 'good relations' is wrong. Apart from being calculated to destroy a lively and dynamic *milieu*, it would tend to attenuate the ever-diminishing Irish opportunities for individual redemption through suffering, poverty, injustice and holy resignation in adversity.

* * *

The Dublin tramsport strike (there's a mistake there but leave it), in reality a crime against soCIEty, is still unsettled. I think one of the difficulties in settling it arises from the fact that nobody knows what the strike is really about. Is it just a question of money? Surely not? True, there is evidence that those morose characters – 'the men' – are worried about the cost of living (leave that too, most of them are fathers!). Quite. But according to an announcement by the Company, the men have no idea of what their jobs are worth. The

Company itself, if it knows the answer, will not reveal it. It simply asks readers of the *Irish Times*, who are frightfully busy people: *Have you reckoned what a Dublin busman's job is worth?* For the present writer's part he can but reply: *No, but apparently not his while.*

Why should anybody's pay be a mystery, an unknown quantity?

The Company says that, in addition to getting some cash every week, the busman is entitled to 'free uniform, free travel to and from work'. If these boons are to be reckoned in computing the worth of a busman's job, why are they called 'free'? Suppose a busman *prefers* to go to and from work on his bicycle? Will he be recompensed for the 'free' bus travel he has no use for?

Of course there is the divil an' all 'free' in addition. There is FREE medical and hospital service, the wife and kids are looked after FREE, there is FREE insurance, a 'relative' who dies is buried FREE, there is – and I am not making this one up! – 'FREE membership of C.I.E. Clubs'. And there is plenty more, and all of it FREE. As if this were not paradise enow I draw attention to the following incredible passage in a letter written by the Company's medical officer:

Two whole-time welfare officers are employed. They are university graduates, fully qualified in social science, and advise and help the employees and their families in domestic problems...

D'you like that? Was there e'er a 'university graduate' in *your* mother's scullery in the ould days solving her 'domestic problems'? Was there, in your youth, this class of conversation ever holden between your good parents –?

THE MA: *Put away that pipe.*
THE DA: *Why?*
THE MA: *The university graduate was here.*
THE DA: *What – again?*
THE MA: *The university graduate says you mustn't smoke before Mollie goes to bed because it might give her an Oedipus complex.*

I do not, I hope, exaggerate. I think it is fair to paraphrase the C.I.E. attitude as follows:

We believe that Life would be far too much for our men. They are incapable of protecting themselves and their families against the ordinary hazards of living. They would be too improvident and foolish to arrange for the important things: we will therefore provide these things in kind and in addition give the men pocket money, hereinafter to be known as their 'pay'.

Frankly lads, I am not sure that we are on the right track here. I believe my doubts are shared by the Rt Rev. Dr Boyd, Bishop of Derry and Raphoe, who was reported as having spoken as follows the other day:

One of the most terrible tendencies of the present time was the growing interference with human personality, and, whenever human personality ceased to be regarded as sacred, there was bound to be retrogression in human conduct and human life . . .

Yes, but the problem is terribly big. It is indeed back of a lot of the social and industrial unrest in Britain today. The worker of today does not want to be 'helped' or patronised – he wants to be paid. He thinks he can manage his own affairs, at work and play. He does not want 'free' playing fields, clubs, canteens, insurance schemes, and so on – particularly where such things come to him from the 'generosity' of his boss. He particularly resents having somebody else pay his income tax for him. The problem is just an aspect of the management mania.

My own opinion? Well, I believe you cannot turn the clock back. Many political communities are now committed to the minute regulation of the lives of their citizens.

An entirely new ethic is being formulated for the twentieth-century humans. Recently this newspaper had a large-type heading as follows:

FINED £50 FOR
FAILING TO SELL
BONELESS HAMS

It wasn't a joke, or a misprint, or anything like that. The heading was a fair summary of a report describing the punishment of crime. One can perhaps imagine a danger arising from boneless hams. It is normal and natural that there should be a bone in a ham; it would probably be a simple matter to prove that the removal of the bone from a ham leads to the growth of bacteria, rendering the meat poisonous, and thus it would probably be fair enough to fine a man £50 for selling meat thus poisoned. But the citizen in question was fined £50 for *failing* to sell boneless hams. Life is going to be terribly complicated and don't say you weren't warned.

Leaving ham, let us return to our muttons. My opinion is this: if we must have paternalism and pauperisation (and I think we must) it should be universal, and whatever is 'free' should be 'free' to everybody who wants it. It should be illegal for any private concern to remunerate its employees otherwise than by money, or to offer them any non-cash inducements. Apart from its larger implications, the thing is as objectionable as truck. Indeed, a transport company which asserts that free transport is part of a busman's wage is probably practising truck, which is quite the word in the circumstances.

I would ask readers, in conclusion, not to blame C.I.E. too much for the list of 'free' boons they have so proudly printed. They did not invent this sort of thing: they dumbly follow a policy which they think is 'modern' and 'enlightened' and wisha, who would begrudge them their warm feeling that they are 'good' employers? If they scrapped all these schemes and distributed the money in wages, the strike would be over tomorrow. (Well, the day after.) They cannot see this – because in my opinion, they are not terribly experienced, highly educated, or suave persons. Only that the word would be a bit comic in a C.I.E. context, I would not hesitate to call the lot of them *arrivistes*!

* * *

I would urge readers to treat with the greatest reserve all they may hear from County Councillors and other Irish mystics on this subject of 'afforestation'. Next to the question of C.I.E. closing down branch lines, 'afforestation' is the favourite theme of ignorant men, no doubt because the great primeval forest is an essential ingredient in the Gaelic Myth – the handiest term I have for the neurotic 'political' desire-dreams which a lot of ye are tormented by today. (By the way, if Freud is right in asserting that adult unhappiness, associated with a refusal to face life for what it is, the pursuit of visions, political elysiums, etc., can be traced to unfortunate childhoods, what on earth was the R.S.P.C.C. doing in Ireland fifty years ago?)

I'm not in the dog business but perhaps I should let you have a few pointers on these matters today? Be safer in the long run, I suppose.

First of all, I shouldn't worry too much about the closing down of branch lines. It is a very Irish notion, building railways for the conveyance of branches. Apart from making very poor fuel branches are too bulky for economic rail transportation: these remote lines represent the slumming fancies of the incompetent former landlord class, and a country that cannot 'afford' to give myself a decent pension (we will say nothing of Alton's unworthy chicanery in connection with the long-promised (God save the mark!) doctorate), such a country certainly cannot afford these open-air rural toys.

The forestry question is a much bigger thing. It must be realised that forests are merely great natural obstacles like mountains and seas, and are thus part of the natural pharmacology which was devised to prevent man destroying himself. Owing to the unfortunately piecemeal method of forest construction (i.e., the use of the tree as a unit) it was possible for man to attack and destroy forests. Were it not for the superior stability of seas and mountains (though when I say that I am not forgetting about our friends, the Americans!), there would no doubt be a great shortage of these same articles today. And it does not take much imagination to bring to mind the proceedings of your excellent parliament in such a situation. The Minister stated that the demolition of mountains was now prohibited, save under licence: four new mountains had been built during the year, three were under construction, and generous grants were available to private persons for the construction of foothills. It was not true to say that the main difficulty holding up the importation of mountains from America was shipping. Plenty of ships were available but sea was rationed by the American authorities. There was a world shortage of sea.

MR DILLON: Fifty years ago there was a sea in Dublin Bay. In those days whole families used to go to what was called 'the sea-side'. I remember the day when, to go to

England, you had to go down to a place called the North Wall *and get into a boat*! Nobody yet knew what Fianna Fáil had cost the country, if 'country' it could now be called. The sale of Knockmealdown Mountains to Portugal was as dirty a transaction as ever came before the House ...

MINISTER: The Deputy's own party advocated it. Perhaps he would now like to have all that rain back?

The Deputy said that the Comeragh Mountains were last heard of in Italy. Blacksod Bay was now bathing millionaires at Palm Beach. They had the Sugarloaf, one of Wicklow's finest mountains, now stored up in the Phoenix Park in a dump, waiting to be sold to God knows what Asiatic tramp. The Department's mountains were a scandal – they were nothing more than molehills, they were already weeping and cracking and wouldn't last twenty years. They had hardly any sea and were down to the last miserable remnant of the natural mountains the country had once been famous for. Outside bedlam, who ever heard of such a travesty of government?

(ANOTHER DEPUTY: In another ten years there won't be a mouse in the country!)

Funny, eh? It's no funnier than the present talk about forestry.

Here is the situation, in brief: it is natural that Ireland should have great forests as well as mountains and seas, but 'natural' only in the sense that primitive and savage conditions of life are preferable to the present 'civilised' order. Take your choice, but you cannot have it both ways. Civilisation is simply the destruction of trees and the substitution therefor of artificial stone shelters: the city simply replaces the forest. Regions where trees are naturally scarce (Greece, Persia, India) are associated with the origins of civilisation, while today in Poland large numbers of people who find a contemporary civilisation unacceptable are known as 'bandits' and are 'roaming the forests' – as in Greece itself, certain 'criminal elements' are stated to be 'in the mountains'.

Of course the tree, like the mountain and the sea, has a mystical significance. A desire for trees, a preoccupation with trees, is a grim atavistic manifestation, a thing of which you highly strung Irish will have to be very careful. Please note that phrase, 'the wild man of the woods'. The tree is historically connected with warfare and bloodshed – for example, in the construction of bows and arrows, of ships (for 'trade', a fancy name for military imperialism) and finally of the gibbet, or *arbor infelix*. (Cf. Arbour Hill.) The tree of knowledge, the tree of life, the family tree, the top of the tree, the tree-top (for sleepy babies) – trees grow thickly in the mind. Why do you name your ships the Irish Elm, the Irish Plane, the Irish Larch, and so on?

I regard this obsession with trees simply as an archaistic indulgence, a love of the past born of a hatred of the present; it is the same thing as the craving to revive ancient languages, customs and dress. You delude yourselves if you think that firewood has anything to do with it. (A Mr Kilmer once thought that he did never see a poem lovely as a tree; it occurs to me that it's a damn pity that poems aren't as useful as trees for putting in the grate, otherwise the fuel situation here would be very satisfactory indeed, and no small thanks to the *Irish Times*.) I don't think your plan to have great forests is *impossible*, mind. But once you have them, the climate and morphology of the country will be utterly changed, and different indeed will be the men who hide in the leafy pleasance of that Silva Gadelica. Why, ye might be even *more* bad-tempered than ye are now! Try the experiment if ye must but leave me out of it (no plantations within ten miles of my house in Santry) and for heaven's sake be careful about lions and monkeys! All I ask is that you first make sure that it would not be cheaper to move the mountains to achieve whatever climatic and social cataclysm ye are after.

With that admonition I make my bough.

Titled Pieces

Trivia Gadelica

The most trivial occurrences dictate the subject of my daily notes here – things seen, half-heard, behaviours and procedures observed, even dull pains in the personal epigastrium; all such impel me toward the study of every aspect of many, many cosmogonies (one million approx.). You remember 'The Fort of Rathangan', Kuno Meyer's translation of an Irish poem?

> The fort over against the oakwood,
> Once it was Bruidge's, it was Cathal's,
> It was Aed's, it was Ailill's,
> It was Conaing's, it was Cuiline's,
> It was Maeldúin's:
> The fort remains after each in his turn –
> And the kings asleep in the ground.

How magical, deep, long and holy is the stream of thought and fancy such lines evoke!

* * *

Last week I read of the death of Bud Fisher, creator of Mutt and Jeff. It brings back the day, long, long ago, when I opened Dinneen's Dictionary at random for the first time, at page 777. It was with mild dismay that my eye encountered 'MUT, anything short'.

'But look here,' I cried out to the walls of my study, 'it's Jeff who's the short one!'

In the lexicon of youth there's no such word as Mut!

* * *

Really, Dinneen will never get his due. The subject may bore some readers, but never the connoisseur of perverted virtuosity. Suppose one looked up an English dictionary to find the exact meaning of 'chair' and found it was 'a yellow worm which infests sandy soil in arid regions; a type of eastern footwear; ale made from gooseberries'. What then?

He has a delightful trick of according to one word meanings precisely contrary. He says *Féine* means: 'the dominant Celtic race-element in ancient Ireland . . . who admitted also churchmen, men of learning, artists and craftsmen; *al*, a farmer, a boor'.

Here are a few more examples. I indicate the normal meaning of each word in brackets:

Grian (sun) – 'The bottom of a lake, well'.

Gealach (moon) – 'The white circle in a slice of a half-boiled potato, turnip, etc'.

Réalta (stars) – 'A mark on the forehead of a beast'.

If you say to somebody *Tá súil agam go bhfuil tú ag dul ar réigh*, it SOUNDS like 'I hope you are making good progress', a kindly sentiment. Dr Dinneen says it means: 'I hope you are about to ascend the scaffold.'

Did I hear you ejaculate 'O!'? Careful! He says *that* means 'ear', and you might be misunderstood as saying 'ear, ear!' Say nothing.

Lunacy

'O, then tell me, Shawn O'Farrall,
    Tell me why you hurry so?'
'Hush, ma bouchal, hush and listen';
    And his cheeks were all a-glow:
'I bear orders from the Captain –
    Get you ready quick and soon;
For the Pats must be together
    At the Rising for the Moon.'

In an article the other day I extolled Ireland's traditional determination to take no part in the world, by which latter term I mean *orbis terrarum*, this earth. And a good job, too, for it makes it all the more unlikely that we will take part in other worlds.

In this particular we are notably unlike a combine one may call the U.S.S.A. Russia and America have announced their intention of engaging in a celestial football match. Rival objects the size of Croke Park Gaelic balls are to be projected so far from the earth that they will encircle the globe for all eternity and, through ingenious apparatus within them, send back a running commentary on the firmament and all its works.

They say that the main objective is to obtain advance information about the weather. I do not believe that, for I did not come down in the last shower. These astral footballs are forerunners of large, inhabited space ships.

* * *

Nobody knows to what purpose such space ships, if they are to be anything more than a *space pthisica*, will be put: not even the makers, I imagine. A number of newspaper writers have been suggesting quite seriously that the day (or night) is at hand when the moon is to be invaded by Homo Sapiens, though it has long been known that the moon is destitute of air and water. Still . . . such obstacles may not be insurmountable. There was hardly any air and no real water on the summit of Everest, yet Hillary and Tensing went there. Imagine the thrill of planting one's flag on the moon, however disastrously one is crippled with moonbite.

As I have suggested, Shawn O'Farrall is unlikely to bother his head about the moon any more than usual, but the moon may bother about him.

* * *

The moon is not one of the nine known planets or moving, as distinct from 'fixed', stars; but if the moon is fair and feasible game for the space-ship marauders, so are the planets. The word planet is from the Greek word *planetes*, a wanderer; apparently nearly home is the wanderer. The last planet, named Pluto, was discovered through the telescope in 1930 by an American in America, and I suppose that gives the U.S. a pre-emptive claim; all they have to do now is lasso the thing or bring it to heel with spatial artillery and declare it one of the United States, conferring upon its inhabitants the right to pursue happiness. (I wonder is there any sinister significance in the fact that one of the atomic raw materials is named plutonium?)

But I repeat my warning to people simple-minded as Shawn O'Farrall, who think the universe might be left as God made it. If the Russians and the Americans start barging about with the heavenly bodies, it is certain that the natural laws heretofore obtaining on earth will be radically altered.

Man-made codes based on them will become quite obsolete – navigation, for instance. Either the tide won't come in at all, or it will come in so fully and with such exuberance that it will drown everybody. The equilibrium which sustains the situation of the heavenly bodies may be so disturbed as to make the earth leave its present orbit, forsake its present status as a planet circling the sun, and become the satellite of some sinister outer planet such as Mars, long reputed to be inhabited by men made of a metallic substance who spend their lives building canals and who would probably kidnap the human race to put them to this work as slaves.

It behoves us all here, in tiny inoffensive Ireland, destitute as we are of any lunatic or interplanetary imperialisms, to be ever vigilant. I have sent the following telegram to Eisenhower: *Very glad you have graciously decided not to interfere with the sun.* – *Myles*.

Odd Thoughts

I think I have made an important discovery which will probably come as a surprise to those (i.e. nearly everybody) who do not realise that they have never seen their own faces and who have no idea what they really look like. My thinking on the subject was provoked by certain 'humorous' remarks I made about a portrait when lecturing at an art exhibition. The portrait was that of a young man sitting on a kitchen chair and having bare feet. I said it was no wonder he had no shoes, that he was obviously poor since the breastpocket of his jacket was on the right-hand side, showing the suit had been turned. Later I met the artist who told me I was wrong; it was a self-portrait and the transposition of the pocket was due to the fact that he was painting from his image in a mirror. This means that a person looking in a mirror sees the face back to front, so to speak.

That is a very important difference because, if a line were drawn vertically down the centre of the face, one half is by no means a replica of the other. There is, in fact, a startling difference. This can be demonstrated by the camera. A fullface picture is taken, and bisected. One half is duplicated by a reversal process and re-integrated with the other half of itself: the result is an entirely different face, with a different expression from the original whole. And if the process is repeated with the other half of the bisected face, we get still a second different face. I am going to ask my friends of the Art Department to see can they let us have this – an original face and the two faces of which it is compounded.

The discovery I mentioned is this – that if you are really anxious to have a good look at your face as others see it (*bonne chance!*) – you can do it by using two mirrors and admiring your reflected reflection, even if at an angle somewhat oblique. However, I cannot quite figure out whether the camera itself makes this reconversion. I don't think so. The lens transposes as does the mirror. I do not see that a print from the negative makes any correction in this regard.

*   *   *

There are many such unsuspected delusions and fallacies in the world – concepts regarded as axioms, things so obviously true that they are in no need of proof or, indeed, so true that they are incapable of proof. I have heard of an American who would not hear of such an attitude. A waiter rushed into a restaurant where this sceptic was eating, shouting 'Coolidge is dead!' Everybody dropped their knives and forks and stared at each other in amazement, but your man went on eating, quite unmoved. He was asked why he took the news so calmly. 'How do you know he is dead?' he asked.

On another occasion, passing a field, a friend with him called his attention to a fine-looking herd of black cattle grazing there. 'This side of them is black,' he said drily.

*   *   *

School children are sometimes punished for not knowing how much are two and two. They are expected to say 'Four'. That is not necessarily a correct answer at all. If two pints of alcohol are mixed with two pints of water, the mixture is less than four pints because of greater molecular cohesion. The contrary is true of other fluids, where $2 + 2 = 4\frac{1}{4}$.

Some social reformer with scientific training should try to invent a new whiskey which, when water is added to it, causes the mixture to contract to nearly nothing.

I would not fancy the job of the barman who would have

the privilege of first serving this potion. Two friends arrive in deep conversation, and order a drink. One has a stout, and the unsuspecting other gets a glass of the new temperance whiskey. Earnestly talking, he adds water generously. His point made, he raises his glass – and then is the atmosphere rent with a cry of pain, shrill as that of a wounded animal.

'*Where's me whiskey gone?*'

There is just a dribble of something in the bottom of the glass. He looks around, glowering. He examines the table to see has he spilled anything. He glares at his friend.

'Did you see me drink anything?'

'No.'

'You didn't . . . I mean to say . . . you didn't swally me drink when I wasn't lookin'?'

'Certainly not.'

'In that case I must be going bats at last. Well, by the godfathers! Hah? Hey, bud!'

Calls barman.

'Now listen here, me boy, I know there's a smell of hay off me, but I didn't come down in the last shower. I paid three-and-sixpence for a glass of malt. I didn't touch what I got. There it is, you can see for yourself. A teaspoonful. Mean to say, I have heard of short measure but this is the blooming limit. Take that glass back and give me what I ordered.'

'Oh, very good, sir.'

It's only after he gets the very same again that the real shooting starts.

The Other Way

I should like to say a word this morning about motor cars. Truth to tell, I am thinking of buying one of the new ones. (*Would Chief Superintendent Michael Farrell, of the Castle, please accept this (the only) intimation?*)

It is most curious how instruments and procedures involving fundamental social change are ignored by the organs, whose function it is to shape and lead. They seem to think it better to follow, to cure rather than prevent. I mean here the

Churches, the schools, even the newspapers. It is not today realised widely enough that the motor is an important social index. You have a car, corduroys, an exhibit at the Living Art show, and you takes your choice.

To go further, serious political adhesions are presumed from car ownership (or should I say custody?). Those Volkswagen yokes have become very popular. But an owner of such a car is naturally presumed by others to be very fond of Goethe and Schiller, and to harbour a secret respect for the German *Zeitgeist*.

* * *

Manufacturers of many articles test public taste from time to time by a process of 'sampling', and make changes and improvements in the articles accordingly. I am not aware that car-makers ever consult the public. But apparently they consult each other, for all modern cars look alike, and are uniform in their ugliness. Changes are made from time to time for the sake of change.

Why, then, not make one's own car? Why not indeed! – yet caution is needed. I once heard of a man of mechanical bent who did so. He hunted through scrapyards and garages for years, picking up odd parts, bits and pieces, so that about forty firms were concerned in the car he finally assembled. It was very handsome, and had not cost much more than £50.

But he had made a slip; he joined the transmission shaft to the top of the back axle assembly instead of to the bottom of it, as the design called for. The car moved all right, but he was dismayed to find on his first trip that he had one gear which would propel the car forward at a spanking 4 m.p.h., while he had four graduated reverse gears. He could drive backwards at seventy miles an hour. Naturally, the steering had also to be reversed in this backward motoring.

It must have been fascinating for his passengers to find themselves sitting with their back to the driver, staring out of the back window – their hearts, no doubt, in their mouths.

* * *

These remarks lead me to mention a most mysterious thing about all present-day cars: I am sure many readers have noticed it. A friend offers you a lift, and you get in beside him. When you reach your destination, you turn the door handle, but the door won't yield to your pressure. Then the oracle at the wheel leans over and says:

'*No: the other way!*'

You shove the handle in the contrary direction, and the door opens. This happens in EVERY car in which you are a guest. If you think you are smart (and you probably do), you remember when trying to get out of car No. 2, that it was to the LEFT the handle should properly be pulled in car No. 1, so you pull No. 2's handle to the left. You are cute. Upon you is a spectacular absence of flies. But the door won't open. And the driver says:

'*No: the other way!*'

Please do not ask me to explain this miracle. It is true, that's all. I seen it. I done it. And there is apparently no remedy. The man who built the car with four reverse gears was simply a foosterer without much real know-how in car engineering. But this door-handle situation is not an engineering phenomenon. It is mystical and suggests that maybe the car-making plants are peopled by saints.

*   *   *

To this day very few cars are powered by a front-wheel drive; indeed, Citroën is the only one which occurs to me off-hand. Yet anybody who has had to deal with a garden roller knows it is far easier to pull the roller than to push it. When you push, you are pushing the roller into the ground, and out of the ground if you pull. Why has this elementary principle not been conceded by the automobile industry in general? It cannot be because of the motor car's ancestry, when it was known as the 'horseless carriage', for the horse was in front of the buggy, and *pulled*.

There is something sinister here, some 'ring' at work, some conspiracy based on the philosophy that inefficiency is more profitable than a job done right. I must come back to the subject another day.

Daily Bread

I hope readers will excuse my recent brief absence due to the necessity of travelling to the White House to discuss with

Mr Eisenhower the complexities of SOTE. (*What!* Mean to say you don't know what SOTE means? These letters stand for State Of The Earth: I break no confidence when I reveal that the condition of that State is Parlous.)

On return to the Emerald Aisle, I read in this paper a thing that surprised, shocked and alarmed me. The headline said: ST KEVIN'S BAKERY TO CLOSE. The quite incomprehensible aspect of this plan was that it was proposed in a report made to the Dublin Board of Assistance by its Chief Executive Officer, Mr Seamus O Murchadha, a gentleman for whom I have the highest respect and esteem. I suppose he is entitled to take leave of his senses occasionally, like the rest of us.

*   *   *

For the information of the wider public it should be made clear that St Kevin's Hospital is merely part of Dublin's mammoth workhouse. The residents – to use a suitably vague term – total something of the order of four thousand persons. Many hundreds are ambulatory and able-bodied. Heretofore this great institution produced most of the bread consumed in its own bakery. The outrageous proposal, already approved, is to close down this bakery and hand over fat wads of the taxpayers' money to the outside bakery cartel.

It is true that a large number of the 'residents' I have mentioned are genuinely destitute, sick or senile, and incapable of work. Every inmate is a hundred per cent charge on the rates, and hundreds are well capable of doing some daily work that would help to pay their passage. One form of work which requires no enormous training or skill is baking bread for intramural consumption. The contention of Mr O Murchadha is that it is cheaper to buy bread from outside 'contractors'. How do you like that?

*   *   *

But here there is a broader issue. It has been much discussed in the British press in recent months, arising from the 'freeing' from Government control of the price of flour and bread. All knowledgeable commentators were agreed that this situation would very shortly entail the extermination of the small local baker and that everybody, like it or lump it, would get an expensive atrocity to be known as the National Loaf. The Dublin workhouse occurrence is fair evidence that the same process is well on the way to becoming a fact in this country.

The public will recall an announcement made a few weeks ago (with a naïveté that was almost endearing) that all bakers' bread contained a carcinomagenic chemical bearing the ludicrous name of agene; the continued use of this poison has been made illegal.

I always try to write only about matters of which I have personal first-hand experience. There is, however, an exception in this case. I think eating bakers' white bread is far too dangerous for persons wishing to sustain life's flame a little longer.

Long-standing Grievance

Do you ever, a chap I know asked me recently, go to the zoo at all?

Not now, I said. *I used to. But they have that place ruinded now what with concrate and 'improvements'.*

I thought to meself, the chap said, that it was a right place to see wild angimals. I put meself on a 10 bus last Thursda. We got held up on the way and do you know be what?

I do not.

Be wild angimals. Tousands and tousands of heifers and bullocks been bet all over the road by angishores and pultogues of drovers from the country, the dumb bastes roarin' out of them from the belting they got from sticks, falling down on their knees and lookin' to make their escape into shops where the people was hidin' with the life terrified out of them. You talk about crulety to angimals!

I know of this, but these unfortunate beasts are not angimals. To be an angimal which evokes human tears here, you have to be a horse. En route for Belgium.

In a Christian counthry, I mane?

Quite.

* * *

Extract from Ulysses, *by J. Joyce, concerning a funeral which took place in June 1904:*

The carriage galloped around a corner: stopped.

—What's wrong now?

A divided drove of branded cattle passed the windows, lowing, slouching by on padded hoofs, whisking their tails slowly on their clotted bony croups. Outside them and through them ran raddled sheep bleating their fear.

—Emigrants, Mr Power said.

—Huuuh! the drover's voice cried, his switch sounding on their flanks. Huuuh! Out of that!

Thursday, of course. Tomorrow is killing day. Springers. Cuffe sold them about twenty-seven quid each. For Liverpool probably. Roast beef for old England. They buy up all the juicy ones. And then the fifth quarter is lost: all that raw stuff, hide, hair, horns. Comes to a big thing in a year. Dead meat trade. By-products of the slaughterhouses for tanneries, soap, margarine. Wonder if that dodge works now, getting dicky meat off the train at Clonsilla.

The carriage moved on through the drove.

—I can't make out why the Corporation doesn't run a tramline from the park gate to the quays, Mr Bloom said. All those animals could be taken in trucks down to the boats.

—Instead of blocking up the throughfare, Martin Cunningham said. Quite right. They ought to . . .

* * *

There you are. It is the duty of the Dublin Corporation to enforce their own public health and sanitary by-laws. Not only are they grossly negligent in that duty but they daily flagrantly contravene them themselves. The zoo might not be a bad place for a public showing of your men the councillors.

Nescience

With the Editor's permission I will reprint a letter which appeared in this paper yesterday. My reason is that it must be looked at carefully, and few people have yesterday's paper at hand. Read this again:

Sir, – Myles na Gopaleen has been retailing extracts from a lady's album which, he says, is about 150 years old and dates from 'about 1800'. It is odd enough that he refers to Lord Chesterfield as being of about the same era. Chesterfield (1694–1773), it is true, said on one occasion, 'Tyrawley and I have been dead these two years; but we don't choose to have it known'; but one would have thought that Mr na Gopaleen would have heard of it by this.

An even stranger feature of this lady's album of 'about 1800', however, is the reference to adhesive postage stamps (first introduced 1840) and railway trains (not in general use until the 1840s). Can it be that Mr na Gopaleen has invented these corny jokes himself?—

Yours, etc.,

THOMAS HOGAN.

Dublin, October 10th, 1954.

Look at that, now! Wrong in matters of fact! who – *me*?

* * *

I have an occupational interest in this sort of thing. I take a deep interest in the pathology of newspaper scribbling. I have spent about fifteen years in this rostrum – should I perhaps call it roastrum? – trying to induce people who write publicly to know what they are talking about, to have achieved mastery of grammar and syntax, to learn how to spell, to verify any matter or word about which they are in the slightest doubt, to wash their literary necks at least once daily – in other words to try to be good Christian Brothers boys.

Nearly all newspaper writing is disgracefully sloppy, even if the slop is sometimes amusing. But, avid as I am to denounce what is sloppy, vague, loose, my vast experience has taught me to view precision with suspicion. How does Thomas Hogan know that Chesterfield's span was '1694–1773'? How can he so aptly quote that Tyrawley witticism?

The answer is simple. He has cogged the whole lot out of the *Encyclopaedia Britannica*.

* * *

That in itself, no great crime. What *is* deplorable is Mr Hogan's obvious unawareness of the perils of quotation. The fundamental peril is the presentation as an unassailable fact of something of which the writer has himself no knowledge whatsoever.

As I have already said here, we certainly live in a strange world if everything asserted in the *Britannica* is true. In this instance, the date given of Chesterfield's birth is completely wrong. Thomas Hogan can find the reason if he has time to inspect the plaque in St Patrick's Cathedral commemorating Dean Swift's servant.

* * *

The other big – and thoroughly reprehensible – thing about this cogging is that the great majority of coggers are incapable of discharging this simple chore accurately; they are incapable of transcribing printed characters accurately. In the *Britannica* version of the Tyrawley joke, there is a comma after 'years'.

* * *

In congratulating Mr E. L. Dawson on his election as President of the Irish Philatelic Society, I am sure he will share my scorn of the allegation that the adhesive was unknown until 1840. (I am quoting when I use the term 'adhesive stamp'; since stamps were first used, it has been found in practice that they are more satisfactory if they adhere to documents to which they have been affixed.) The year 1840 is known even to ignoramuses as the year in which Rowland Hill introduced the penny post.

* * *

My statement that Chesterfield 'could be said to be a man of that era' (*c.* 1800) is a matter of fact. I did not use the word century. Apart from that, the extracts I gave from the albums of the Unknown Woman were directed to showing the astonishing tranquillity of many departments of social life at a time when collective mankind was in ferment. Anybody who has read the ludicrously dignified writings of Chesterfield would imagine that he was a retired old gentleman from birth, never summoning so much courage even as to go for a walk. In fact he had a most turbulent life, including an intervention in Irish politics.

Thinking similarly, I would not be surprised to know that the gentle maiden who compiled those albums was the Mrs Warren of her day.

* * *

Mr Hogan questions my reference to railway trains. Here we are back to this incapacity to read. I had no reference whatsoever to railway trains, and no hint whatsoever about steam locomotion. The album had mention of 'railways'. Railways were used by Hannibal.

The disclosure that (steam) railway systems were not in general use until the 1840s will bring a tired smile to old steam men in general. The centenary of the opening of a steam railway system between Dublin and Cork was celebrated in 1952 by the running of a ceremonial train laden with guests.

How am I so sure of the year? Because I drove the engine.

In Hopsital

Many years ago, when I was younger and in digs in Rathmines *sub auctoritate* Mrs Paw-Nay, I had one night something which I had thought peculiar to ill-oiled internal combustion engines – a seizure. 'It is what we call,' I heard Mrs Paw-Nay confide to a shawly visitor in the kitchen, '*yoon convoolsiyoon*. The heatrt is choked wid the black biiile and I wouldn't mind oney I warnded and I counter-warnded that boy from puttin' crabs in his gob bought off that basketmen creeonyomils from Clogherhead in the Stolen Six Counties.'

More betoken, she caused to be summoned for my use a machine which she called an 'ambunals', and soon I was in a Dublin hospital, looking at a nurse who held me tenderly by the wrist.

* * *

Of course that was years ago, when medicine and even sickness was in its infancy. I remember that during the first night I developed, in addition to the initial crab syndrome, a ferocious boil on the back of my neck; this compelled me to adopt a peculiar nodding and acquiescent attitude in the bed. But my bould nurse was very observant; nothing escaped her owlish eagle eye. She brought me a bowl of a lukewarm, cloudy medicament, which I dutifully swallowed. Then she brought me on a tray certain grey poultices for my unfortunate sore neck. I stopped her on her next round of mercy.

'Nurse,' I said (rather testily, I admit), 'you have brought me no bandages. How do you expect me to apply these poultices to my neck?'

'Smart boy wanted,' she said coarsely. 'That's your breakfast. Ate it and shut your gob.'

This, to use slang parlance, 'shook' me.

'What was that dose you gev me earlier?' I asked. 'Was it veetameens or an anti-tetanus mixture?'

'Do you hear him?' she said, appealing to my neighbour in the next bed, an unfortunate character who appeared to have tertiary leprosy. 'What do you make of a jem that doesn't know shavin' water when he sees it?'

I recall that I had one visitor that day. I think her name was Miss F. Nightingale.

Halcyon days! Brave days! Not a Sunday passed but we had roast *poulet halcyon* for dinner, garnished with poultice pudding and roost potatoes. (Yes, irrepressible old dogs that we were we DID call them roost potatoes, uncertain whether they were eggs or spuds, fried in metal filings. And how we afterwards boasted of our iron constitutions!)

*   *   *

Nowadays, thank goodness, all that is changed. Should I say, though, *all* that? Gob, I don't know. I am charitable and I make my rounds faithfully to see my ailing contemporaries frail as I am nowadays to be encargoed with bags of oranges, *Illustrated*, sweets, half-pints, butter, honey, and tiny, ornate jars of sodium amytal gr. iii. I am afraid they have all one complaint. And it is an old one.

It sent me to the library in my place in Santry. Sure enough, I found what I was seeking. At the turn of the century the students in St Bartholomew's Hospital, London, had a little magazine to which they contributed sundry witty inventions in verse and prose. Most of them, alas, are of the inferior order. But the statement of one poem is, I fear, still valid. So, at least, my sick friends affirm.

*   *   *

The name of the author, cowardly enough, is 'Anon'. I had better quote his poem which is called 'The Night Nurse' –

> Who is it comes – a perfect pest –
> At six a.m. to break my rest,
> Disturbing me in my warm nest?
>   The Night Nurse.

Who draws my locker to my bed,
And puts thereon both tea and bread,
And says 'Wake up! You sleepy head!'?
    The Night Nurse.

Who to remove superfluous dirt,
A basin brings with orders curt,
'Sit up and wash – take off your shirt'?
    The Night Nurse.

Who bustles round till half-past eight,
Dusting at a terrific rate,
And scolding if the least bit late?
    The Night Nurse.

Who goes when things are all put right,
And leaves me grinning with delight,
But dreading still the coming night?
    The Night Nurse.

Ye who are sick and depressed – take heart. Learn that poem. And when she comes on duty, calm, starched, minatory, *chant* it in unison.

That'll larn her.

Standing A Loan

My friend Dr Lennox Robinson, who has been writing in another paper, recently announced wryly that it's time to give up since, after a year and a possible total of perhaps 80 articles, he was bound to start repeating himself. The announcement of the £20 million loan issues prompts me to tell a perfectly true little story about money. I *may* have told it before but don't think so; even if I have I will accept censure only from persons who never themselves repeat a story. I think that proviso makes me pretty safe.

I see, incidentally, that Dr Robinson intends to dedicate a plaque in memory of Oscar Wilde in Westland Row next Saturday; I presume it is an outdoor plaque. I am *not* going to repeat the objections I have already set out to this enterprise, but I do hope that the police will see to it that this narrow and extremely busy thoroughfare is not obstructed. I reserve my own right to arrive in an enormous six-wheel lorry. And now for our story.

* * *

Some years ago I was having a drink with a friend in a Dublin pub. We were seated in a small snug which gave a full view of the inside of the counter. There we sat, talking wittily, drinking and resting ourselves.

After a while, my friend found his money was exhausted and that his cheque book was in his office. He asked me to lend him a few pounds, I found I had three, and readily gave him two.

That sounds reasonable so far, I hope.

But I reflected that my friend was a well-to-do and open-handed person, and that two pounds would not carry him very far. So I produced my own cheque book.

'Listen,' I said, 'I think I'd better give you some more to keep you going, particularly if you're really thinking of going to the Curragh?'

He said all right, if it was convenient.

So I wrote in his favour, correctly signed and dated, a cheque for One Million Pounds. He examined it and, when ordering the next drink, said to the curate:

'Paddy, I've a cheque here and want a few quid for the races. I don't want it all now – just hand me out ten, and keep the cheque for the present.'

'Sairtintly,' the curate said, taking the cheque and walking up with it to the 'piana' (as cash registers are called). I watched him very closely. He stood eyeing the cheque, his hand poised aloft to register a NO SALE. A blush of anger began to suffuse his neck and face. Then he walked back to the two Excellencies in the snug, scowling heavily. He pointed to the cheque.

'Are you trying to get me into a row with the boss?' he barked.

'No. Why?' we said innocently.

'This thing isn't endorsed,' he roared.

* * *

My friend had many weeks' diversion with that cheque. Its constant presentation in public houses, however, made inroads on its physique. One day he showed it to me, frayed and ripping at the crease.

'Give me that cheque,' I said. I tore it up and again produced my own cheque book.

'You must remember,' I said, 'that the cost of living has gone up a lot since I wrote that last cheque.' So I gave him a new cheque, this time 'not exceeding one million and a half pounds sterling'.

And there was nothing illegal in any of this carry-on. Try it for yourself!

Chronitis

The other day I went – *à la recherche du temps perdu*, perhaps – into my old office, the Scotch House; the place once wittily I had called Grandeur de Foley. I sampled a bottle of ginger wine, gingerly. I will be honest and confess I felt a bit depressed; began thinking of making my wall (*stet* – there won't be any loop-holes in it, not that I believe in keeping loops in holes), and worrying. Yes, *worrying*. About myself, my writings, my poetry, my future. You see, I have the impression of having been here a long time, yet do not seem to be growing old enough. Extraordinary complaint if you like but I have no corns or ulcers and I am still encountering things which are *quite new* to me. Surely this is embarrassing immaturity and damn the thing else? Am I inexperienced? Callow? Or is this . . . innocence?

This, em, pulse known as time – 'the experience of duration' – is still very baffling, notwithstanding the expositions and expostulations of men such as Minkowski, Einstein, Eddington. A horse has one-third the life expectation of a man. If a man is riding a horse, what sort of time informs this association? One reads that Newton distinguished two kinds of interval distinguishing events – distance in space and lapse in time. But what is it that lapses? The time–space men confute Newton and say there is in fact one interval. Do you know, it would put years on a man.

* * *

I had all this disquiet many space-years ago on another visit to the Scotch House, sent for Foley and explained my difficulties to him. I did not feel *quite* mature, I said, and might well be misleading *Irish Times* readers on matters philosophical, eschatological, even political: even such a suspicion would induce in me a socratic dementia and a demand for a large *pharmakon* and baby soda. I would have to find some method of accelerating time and growing older and wiser quicker. It was useless fooling about with systems of dynamic or kinematic time, or worrying about the sudden space accretions which might be involved in a successful acceleration of time. Mature more rapidly I must, I told Foley, and I thought there was only one remedy: would he put me into bond?

Refused, said he hadn't an empty bin in the place. I knew I had to think up some other method of senescing. Time was not everything but the time factor was most important.

* * *

It happened, indeed, that I knew him well in those days. It happened there was a strike on below at the North Wall in the Dublin port – there was a lot of time being imported for building contracts and even some time-and-a-half for the dockers. Do you know what happened? It went bad. The mairrchints, of course – the usual thing – wanted to blame it on the time factor. The time factor washed his hands of the whole thing, said his contract ended at Dublin quay and that he'd have to be paid. The mairrchints said it would have to go to arbitration. The time factor invoked the war clause. At the heel of the hunt after hopping and trotting he got paid. But the mairrchints took it real bad and there was talk of them sending over direct to Greenwich in future.

But that's neither here nor there – this stuff that went bad nothing would do the Port and Docks oney refuse to collect it, said there was no provision in the rates for wet time.

Can you beat it? Thirty-eight-odd bob in the pound in rates and that's the thanks you get! Better off under the British how are ye – if you ask me we were better off under the *Danes*!

Any reader with time on his hands might send me some. I'm serious!

Boredom

Six chambers? A small country house? A *bijou* establishment with six chambers? Each containing a pullet? I have all that, but the first letter of the last word in the preceding sentence is *wrong*. (It's that printer again! This war has been going on for so many years that I have included his blood in my will! What the widow is going to do with it is another matter, but I can see Mr Justice Conor Maguire – or is Michael Killanin the present head – gravely shaking the head. *We can't have anything to do with the blood of any man who changes Myles's prose. It wouldn't be safe to inject that stuff into anybody*.)

I can hardly quarrel with the sentiment. But what is added by 'into anybody'?

* * *

After this portentous exordium, I should like to say that the six-chambered apartment is no hotel, although the idea of quietus might not be irrelevant; it is a gun. It is possible that I will use it shortly. With a few associates, I met recently with The Man Who Forgot He Told You That Story Yesterday.

I won't ask the reader whether he has ever met this type. He could never have forgotten the experience.

* * *

Let us quietly devise a notional situation. Here, for instance, is the story, witty, very brief.

Eve was made from a rib taken from Adam. One evening Adam stole away from the Garden of Eden. Eve was suspicious. When he came back and fell asleep, she counted his ribs.

That is our text. There are five of us in the smokeroom and we are all, naturally, commercial travellers. We are having coffee and, perhaps, an odd small one. Most of us have manners on us, and would not be deliberately rude to a fellow mortal. *He comes in!*

He beams on us. I heard a very good one last night, lads, he says. (*We* had, too – from him.) This is one of the best I have heard for a long time. Wait till you hear.

The face breaks into a slow, anticipatory, crackling smile; water comes from the eyes: the appalling tragedy begins:

'There's nothing irreverent about this, lads, believe me. It's about . . . Adam and Eve . . .'

By this time, of course, the 'lads' have exchanged glances: and very deadly glances, some of them, each saying *why haven't you the guts to tell him to shut up?*

* * *

'Now I want to bring your minds back to the Garden of Eden. You may have heard of our First Parents. I know you are not exactly the type that goes in for that sort of thing, but I am going to make this very simple and short . . .'

Still nobody has the courage to make even a perfunctory protest, not even when he begins to indulge in prefatory private laughs.

'You know about Eve being made from Adam's rib? That's really the whole point of the story. If you miss that, you miss the whole story. Do you get me, lads?'

Yes, the lads get him all right, but they are thinking of getting him in quite another way, perhaps with shot-guns.

* * *

Here is the appalling end to my story. I have already told that little Adam and Eve Story here! *Cuss quistodiet?*

City Haul

Rumour has reached my ears that I am retired. It is quite wrong and probably malicious: I have been merely tired resting myself in the house of the married sister in Skerries. People there, having looked at each other, ask who is yon man paddling out four yards on the great strand, the faded flannel trousers folded up to the knee? I told youngsters who were young enough to ask myself the question direct that I was Santa Claus; they had never heard the name and later saluted me as Mr Claus. Maybe Mr Claws would be nearer the mark.

Certain parties and factions have been taking impudent advantage of my absence from the public rostrum. Witness the recent prodigious essay in cheek by members of the Dublin Corporation, who ordained by a majority vote (17–7) that a report from consultants saying that the Corporation apparatus is scandalously wasteful should not be made available to the excruciated ratepayers; furthermore, that the same firm should not be employed for a closer probe into this corrupt and vicious organisation.

Two members of the City Council, Messrs Finnegan and Mullen, demanded its publication. They were overruled.

* * *

The consultants' report (as reported) isolated several points of administration where there was serious waste of public money. Last Friday our own Political Correspondent of this paper wrote an article on the report which made it clear (I say this with all respect to our correspondent) that he has not seen the report but based his discourse on what he was told by 'senior officials'. What else would those boys do but exculpate themselves?

Public bodies in this country are hopelessly corrupt, the more so by reason of the Management Acts. Officials are easily blamed but they are night and day besieged by the 'elected representatives' to get jobs for their go-boys. Fifty years ago it was a sort of dirty joke to say that all you had to do to get work was to go upstairs in Kavanagh's Wine Rooms and see Long John Clancy, carrying your fare (a couple of fivers) in your fist. Things are still much the same. With the impact of unemployment and emigration, jobs have become more precious than ever before, and the impulse to get 'a few days' is much stronger. The idea (and sound enough it is) is that, once in, you will take a lot of shifting.

I need hardly add that not all Corporation employees are of that class; but far too many of them are. To repeat myself – the ratepayer foots the bill for the whole lot. I am myself a ratepayer and am sick and tired of the whole game. Its basis is political chicanery.

A long time ago, the position was much the same. Mr W. T. Cosgrave fired the whole Corporation and appointed three men to do their work. This was before managerial dispensation, but the triumvirate in no time slashed the rates and fired a swarm of wasters, tipplers, touchers and gobhawks who had been quartered on public funds.

* * *

To this situation there is a sinister overtone. I mention it as a possibility. No local authority can do anything without the 'sanction' of the Department of Local Government Board, apart from threatening people and keeping urban streets in a filthy condition. It is reasonable to assume that this lodge was consulted about the present shemozzle in the Corporation and condoned and approved it. They have as much respect for a human being as for the mountain goats with whom they were reared. Is this civilisation?

You can search me.

Clothes Line

There is an ancient witticism concerning two drapers in a small town who were bitter rivals. One day the more enter-prising draper erected a screen of sacking over his fascia board, and painters began to work behind this screen. The villagers gawked and wondered what was going on. One fine morning the sacking was removed, and there, in large brilliant letters, was this motto:

MENS SANA IN CORPORE SANO.

The rival draper was dismayed, but by no means beaten. He, too, erected a hoarding of sacks. Public curiosity became almost hysterical. When, eventually, the sacks were taken down it was clear that the second contender had won easily. The motto which the astounded townspeople saw was this:

MEN'S AND WOMEN'S SANA IN CORPORE SANO.

If this anecdote proves anything, it proves that drapers are important people, and that clothing maketh the full man.

*   *   *

I wish to say a word about men's clothes. The average man wears wool, linen, leather, felt, rubber, metal, celluloid, and, perhaps, poplin. He wears these materials on particular parts of his person and nowhere else. Why this unenterprise? Felt is always worn on the head (the affair is called a hat) but why never a pair of felt trousers? What is wrong pray with a fancy waste-coat made of rubber? It is not true to say that a leather tie would last for life and should be washed from time to time with a lick of a sponge? (Would dribblers please note?) Alas for the day of the Man in the Iron Macs!

* * *

The foregoing may seem a bit facetious, but I will tell you of something that is no laugh at all. I mean the pockets in men's trousers. They are the most used part of any suit. Not only are they used for carrying coins, keys and other oddments; they also for long periods carry hands, and are used, not only as receptacles, but often as organs of gesture – often extremely violent gesture. The ramming of hands fiercely into trouser pockets, accompanied by grotesque distortion of the shoulder structure, is often a most explicit manifestation of what one thinks of Mr Eamon de Valera, T.D.

I say as a fact that, quite irrespective of what one pays for a suit, there will be holes in the trouser pockets within a fortnight of continuous wear. Other matters apart, our system of pricing ensures that our pockets contain fabulous quantities of pennies, halfpennies and threepenny bits. The weight of all this alone must have a seriously adverse effect on the durability of our footwear.

Twenty years ago the trouser pockets of the cheapest suits were made of canvas, and were still intact long after the suit had wasted away. All pockets of today are made apparently from cheap Egyptian cotton. It is my submission that human beings are entitled to pockets not inferior in quality to those of a snooker table.

Would the Master Tailors kindly note? Let them stop loafing and lunging, take their hands out of their pockets and get down to work.

Bankrupture

The situation arising from the action taken by the bank staffs is, according to one's viewpoint, either most interesting or most lurid. I am advised that it has already caused a minor run on the banks, for people in a large way of business will not risk repetition of the 1950 *trahison des clercs*, as they probably called it. That stoppage, however, was due to a strike. If the banks were to retaliate in the present circumstances with a lock-out, it seems such action would amount to repudiation of their contractual obligations to customers. That way lies trouble.

The attitude of the officials is not without an element of the naïve. They say: 'We are not as well off, earnings per hour, as we were in 1938.' Who is, bar certain speculators, tycoons and criminals?

It is possible that they have not given sufficient weight to two important considerations. The first is that the financial load on most people increases as they grow older. Old age and hard times are companions. That life is a tedious fraud becomes more apparent with every year that passes. What industrial organisation can be expected to provide for a man's whiskey being secretly drunk by his wife and his rake of a son?

* * *

The second reason is more physical than financial. Any person who was employed in a bank in 1938 is today fifteen years older. This may entail ulcers, sclerotic decomposition of the nervous system, vascular empyema, or merely psychopathic addiction to pokeweed; thus calls for revision of pay may really amount to the cry 'Give us back our youth!'

It should be remembered, too, that bank proprietors and directors are also fifteen years older than they were in 1938. Mellower? Genialler? More replete with the milk of human kindness? I don't think so.

And what of those who were not working for the banks at all in 1938?

* * *

The root and branch (particularly branch) of this whole problem is, of course, the preposterously large number of banks which operate in this little land – only the Twenty-Six Counties are involved – and their profligately costly methods of operation. A town of any size has three or four branches of different banks trading under a system of strict non-competition with each other, with three or four officials in each branch. Probably the severest example of this unique business methodology is to be found in Dublin. One of the banks has a branch on the Rathmines Road. It is a very busy thoroughfare, and a nervous person might fear for life and limb in crossing the road; but this bank, ever solicitous for the safety of its clients, *has another branch of itself right opposite.*

Worse, the State itself has only the most tenuous control of the conduct of the country's financial structure. Mr Sweetman has yet to show his mettle, but it is true to say that no person who has occupied the post of Minister of Finance *ab urbe condita* has shown the slightest knowledge of the science of money. What is called the Central Bank of Ireland is a pitiful sham. It collects statistics, issues 'Irish' notes imported from a British printer, and publishes an annual report spelt out in the most fearsome English; it performs none of the major tasks proper to a central bank, such as does the Banque de France.

How about us all becoming culcidarians? *Culcida* is the Latin for mattress.

Natotion

I am no student of political affairs. (I apologise for allowing the Dublin man in me to break out; I begin again.) I am no student of political affairs. I take the short cut, study politicians instead, and get there sooner. This morning I have the honour to report that a certain Irish statesman is not feeling too well in himself at all. And who is he when he is at home? you ask. Chap name of Lord Brookeborough. Decent type.

How do I know that he is on edge, uncertain, even *afraid*? I wrote to him some months ago asking him to give me an interview, saying I was not intent on any 'exposure' or 'scoop'; I added even that I would show him in advance the text of what I meant to publish. A polite secretary replied saying that this interview was not possible. You can make bacon of that.

If the Lordship was afraid that I would raise with him the 'problem' of partition or his own preposterous pretence that he is some sort of a Scotchman or Britisher instead of a decent paddy like the rest of us, he could rest aisy. As a guest, it would be discourteous of me to question of the validity of the household gods neatly arranged on the mantelpiece.

This partition nonsense does not worry me at all. The arrangement will decay and disappear with comic abruptness like, e.g., the Westminster improvisations in Suez and Cyprus. Did you ever hear a couple of thousand people cheering with a Northern accent? *I* did. They were cheering a crowd of gurriers who had arrived uninvited during the Belfast blitz on machines marked DUBLIN FIRE BRIGADE. And you can make bacon of that too.

*   *   *

Partition is, however, of some transitory importance inasmuch as it is the reason given by Republican stetsmen (*state!*) for not having the country a member of NATO. This NATO is the mechanism devised to protect Western Europe from the Kremlin hoodlums, from whom the Irish have rather more to fear than others; they might be deprived even of their traditional poverty. With Britain now a bought-and-paid-for U.S. satellite, it is possible that the East–West collision will actually occur on these islands, and this 'neutrality' card will not successfully be played a second time. Can Irishmen north or south afford these obsolete affectations? Is it safe to be cut off from the rest of Europe, to be literally so insular, islanded. Is it even *possible*?

I report that it is. Read on.

*   *   *

In a pub last week I met a real Dublin man. As his cap and steel 'key' betokened, he was out of the Corporation Waterworks, and I got talking to him about his experiences. But let him speak for himself.

'There comes a call wan mornin' that there was a waterburst in Talbot Street. Near the Pillar, you know, and very heavy traffic. Meself and three other lads was sent down with a hancar in charge of Mr —— that was in charge of another job above in Rutland Square. He markeded out the place on the road, told us to get busy and then went off on his bike to see about the other job. We opened up the road and got well down, but the water was still comin'. He come back in an hour and wants to know what all the delay is about. One of the lads showed him a big pipe that was in the way halfway down.

'Cut that —— thing out of your way, find this leak and stop this nonsense,' says he. The lads ripped this earthing-ware pipe affair out of the way, found the leak another foot down, stopped it and then sewn up the road. But there was sacred holy melia murder about it afterwards. Know what the pipe was?'

I truthfully said I did not.

'Th' Atlantic cable!'

The Waterman*

I told yesterday about my meeting with the Dublin Water-works man and how he and his friends accidentally severed the Atlantic cable while looking for a leak under 'Talbot Street'. I continue my report of our conversation but would emphasise that he was a real Dublin man, slightly sad – perhaps 'resigned' is a better word – and quite incapable of being surprised by anything. His speaking voice lacked all inflection.

'When you open a road,' he said reflectively, 'you never know what you're going to come across. I seen bones and human skeletons and in wan place a load of bran new coppers dated nineteen and o two. Ah yes. And any godsamount of swords and small hatchets.'

He drank half of his pint effortlessly and looked (as I thought) *through* the wall. Then he said:

'Do you know the 100-Ton Crane?'

It seemed a warm, gentle question like 'Do you know Glendalough?' or 'Do you really believe there's a God in heaven?' I correctly caught the mood.

'*A personal friend*,' I said briefly.

* * *

'There come a call wan day that there was a waterburst down

---

* An asterisk at the title of an article means, and will henceforth mean, that the article is absolutely true and that any incredible statement in it has been, where possible, verified.

the kays. Four lads were went down with a hangcar. And a bar and hammer. It's a stone street.'

'*A stone street?*'

'Yaaa. Setts.'

'*I see.*'

'This butty of mine put the bar in between two setts and begun to sledge it. He was sledgin' there for ten minutes, and the bar gun down about two fut. He then drawn back to give it another wallop when – PPFFWWTTT! – the bar flun up about a quarter of a mile in the air and come down in the —— Liffey.'

He paused and gazed with a long expression of piety into his empty glass. I said nothing, and showed no interest whatever in the story. A question here on my part would have been an inexcusable lapse from taste.

'AFTER THAT THE 100-TON CRANE WOULDN'T MOVE.'

I pondered this masterly disclosure in silence. Then I risked making the correct reply. I spoke very casually, and I think the remark passed.

'*A lucky man,*' I said, '*that he wasn't electrocuted.*'

* * *

'Wan day a few year ago wan of your crowd in th' *Irish Times* got one of the lads into trouble. He was mindin' his own business listenin' for leaks when this foretographer come along. Wanted to know what my butty was up to with the key at his ear. How did he know a leak was a leak and how did he know where the leak was leakin' and all this class of yap out of him. And would he mind posin' for a pitcher. It was more to get shut of this foretographer that your man said he would. When the pitcher come out in th' *Irish Times*, he was sent for above in th' office. This engineer asks him did he know the pitcher was taken and did he pose for it and did he think he was paid out of the rates for been an *Irish Times'* foretographer's module. Ah . . .?'

I did not like this manifestation of petty tyranny and said so. I asked him for the engineer's name. He shrugged and said it did not matter as the man was now retired. He then made what I think is a very profound remark:

'What am I talkin' about? I'm wrong. He's not retired. He's dead.'

Organising Ruin

The destruction of Dublin, an ancient city, is a matter of public concern; my use of that word 'destruction' need not invoke horror-thoughts of bombing. By it I mean the menace of unlicensed and unrestricted shopkeepers. This thing I complain of has taken the form, within the last twenty years or so, of the exploitation of an amenity of building which has cost, apart from the initial cost of labour and erection, the passage of up to two centuries of something humans have no control over: I mean time.

This thing should have been stopped at least ten years ago. The main thoroughfares – let us say from the top of Grafton Street via O'Connell Street to the Parnell Monument – are a shrieking honky-tonk of neon lights. The lights demand far higher consumption of cigarettes and ice cream, emphasising occasional skyline reminders that it is easy enough to go to America. Here we have the Gaelic Babylon. May God help us!

*   *   *

There are two recreants here: the one is the Town Planning Committee of the Dublin Corporation, and the other is the Department of Local Government Board. There is no planning whatsoever in Dublin. The two authorities I have mentioned have reasonably competent staffs, but the sort of work they have to do is again and again made null either by municipal intrigue or political chicanery. The city will wear on its face for centuries the scars. Would it not be better, in the interest of our ancestors and successors – to say nothing of us now here – to see to it that the persons I have mentioned, are flung out, one and all, body and soul?

The new concrete-box sub-cities such as have been perpetrated at Ballyfermot and Crumlin are outrages. The pressure brought on Corporation officials in connection with the allocation of new tenancies is so insanitary a twilight that I will not invite the reader to accompany me into it today.

*   *   *

But there is another body who must share guilt in this ghastly process of permanently mutilating Dublin city. I mean the architects. You do not have to go into an exhibition of outrageously bad pictures, but nobody who has eyes can fail to see the atrocities which have been perpetrated in the city streets, as to design, construction and décor. In terms of mere external paint, a hue commonly associated with dysfunction of the gall bladder has become the Thing.

Those architect chaps will say: 'Well, what the dickens can we do? We are only obeying a client's instructions.' I can say that that last sentence is not true. Your businessman necessarily stipulates the accommodation he needs in a new or reconstructed building and may lay down a maximum cost figure, but he attempts no architectonic dictation.

* * *

Those of us who are of full age will remember what Mr William T. Cosgrave did with a Dublin Corporation as incompetent as the one that is there today; he fired the lot and installed a triumvirate who did a most spectacular job in cleaning up. At least one of these gentlemen is to this day giving distinguished service in a major public job.

It is the clear duty of the present Minister in the Customs House to do what Mr Cosgrave did. I warn him to attend to this matter. I warn him not to confuse Dublin city with the stone townlands of Donegal.

Public Money

Where would writers like me be were it not for offensive organisations and public nuisances such as C.I.E., Boord Fawlthah, the Abbey Theatre, the N.U.I., R.G.D.A.T.A., the U.S., the Garlic Leak and et cetera. A bottle of stout can be sold with a fair profit for eightpence; most publicans charge tenpence. A reader reports that a bottle of stout on the C.I.E. train ex Cork cost 1s 2d. That is a scandalous and extortionate charge. He left a coat and case in the cloakroom at Cork, for which service he had to pay a shilling. The same service at Amiens Street cost 6d.

Mr Frank Lemass, General Manager of C.I.E., has been speaking to accountants at Limerick. He said it was fallacious to conclude that because C.I.E. was losing money, it was operating inefficiently. The public who have to use the

Dublin bus services are in no need of financial reveries to know that these services are grossly inefficient.

Nor is there any loss on those services; on the contrary there is a considerable profit, no doubt now of staggering volume as a result of the last increase in fares and the deliberate and vicious manipulation of stages which makes many familiar journeys of a few hundred yards cost 4d. The fruits of this exorbitant fare structure are channelled off to subsidise the trips of the turnip-snaggers to the fields down the country and also, of course, to pay for the great fleet of staff cars. The upper clerks of C.I.E. should, if horrified at the idea of relying on the buses, get to their offices on scooters bought by themselves.

* * *

The Abbey Theatre causes much more amusement than it provides, though perhaps amusement is not the word. It is a sort of National Sore, continually presenting the Irish people as even worse cornerboys than they are, in plays written by thullabawns and often presented by peasants who do not disdain the ultimate effrontery of pretending that they are *acting* peasant parts. Even in the distant days when the theatre had some dignity, it produced no playwright of note but did develop considerable actors and actresses.

The recent Dáil Erin debate on the Abbey was funny all right. Mr Moloney (Feena Fayl) said 'its directors were men of outstanding integrity, ability and good national background'. In due course we should consider having this assembly's jokes televised.

The managers of other theatres proper and theatre-cinemas which have no public subsidy have complained of hard times but acknowledge help in overall income from catering services, the sales of sweets and ice cream, and from the bars. The Abbey does not sell ice cream at all (presumably because it is favoured by teddy boys and teenagers and unheard of by bogmen) and, as for its bar, it opens only at the intervals and, in a three-act presentation, closes for good at the second interval. A customer, infuriated by a wretched play, cannot retire to the bar for a cup of coffee or a different drink.

So long as the Abbey gets thousands every year in State

subsidy, its accounts should be minutely examined by the Controller and Auditor-General. I need hardly express my hearty concurrence with the protests made in the Dáil against handing this gang £250,000 of public money on a plate. The proposal was put forward by Mr O. Traynor, Minister for Justice. Mr Traynor is nearly seventy-four years of age. He should resign.

*   *   *

British European Airways have put out a multicoloured leaflet describing the cities they serve. Dublin Castle is described as 'residence of the former English viceroys' and the production adds that if you go at the right time 'you can enjoy Ireland's Eisteddfod – the A t'-Oireachtas'.

I received several begging letters in connection with that peasant hooley. They contained numerous mistakes in grammar.

Fossilanguage

The year 1906 occurred some fifty years ago. How long ago that is may be gathered from a remark made in a Gaelic League paper – I translate: 'It appears that the Emperor of Russia is getting some sense into his head at last. It is stated that he intends to found a democratic Parliament based on the will of the people of that unfortunate country.'

But in certain other respects, times have not changed at all. I have been looking at a little book published in 1906; it is by an American, Gelett Burgess, and deals with 'bromides', clichés, and the like. The years have in no way impaired their ghastly bloom. And remember – what had become a cliché by 1906 must have been developing its petrifaction for many a year before that, so that we are really dealing in centuries. Let me quote some samples from Mr Burgess.

*   *   *

I don't know much about Art but I know what I like.

That dog understands every word I say.

It isn't the money, it's the *principle* of the thing I object to.

No, I don't play chess. I haven't that kind of brain.

Funny how some people can never learn to spell.

It's bad enough to see a man drunk – but *a woman*!

It's a mistake for a woman to marry a man younger than herself – women age so much faster than men. Think what she'll be when he's fifty!

Of course, if you happen to want a policeman, there's never one within miles of you.

Come up and see us any time, now that you know where we are. You'll have to take pot-luck but you're always welcome.

Did you ever know of a famous man's son who amounted to anything?

I haven't played a game of billiards for two years but I'll try, just for the fun of the thing.

He's told that lie so often that he now believes it himself.

* * *

There are many more of a like quality, all vigorously alive today. Mr Burgess offers a brief pathological annotation, instancing this remark:

If you saw that sunset painted in a picture, you'd never believe it would be possible.

'It must be borne distinctly in mind,' he says, 'that it is not merely because this remark is trite that it is bromidic; it is because that, with the Bromide, the remark is inevitable. One expects it from him and one is never disappointed. And moreover it is always offered by the Bromide as a fresh, new, apt and rather clever thing to say. He really believes, no doubt, that it is original – it is, at any rate, neat, as he indicates by his evident expectation of applause.'

* * *

My Gaelic overlordship cannot resist – what if not the temptation to record here and now rather than there and then a few other examples which time and again rear their ugly head:

War is a biological necessity.

Gin is a very depressing drink.

If I had a good book I wouldn't dream of going out at night at all.

There is only one thing for a cold – stop in bed.

Half of those houses with television aerials have no sets.

There's nothing as refreshing as a good cup of tea.

In another year or two you'll see people having breakfast in Dublin, lunch in New York, and supper back in Dublin.

(Come into my brackets for a moment. Why must we be expected to undertake these perilous rocketings across the heavens merely to eat in strange hemispheres? Would not lunch in Ballybrophy be equally dissimilar to lunch at home – at least for non-residents of Ballybrophy? And in any event, if one has got to the stage of having lunch in New York, what possible pretext is there for going back to Dublin after lunch? Why not have supper in Bombay?)

Did you notice, by the way, that there is a great stretch in the evenings?

The Small Lads

I remember a Dublin landlady who once put me up (and with whom up I had to put) often reproving me sternly for my habit of taking the skin off boiled potatoes in thick crude slashes of the blunt knife I had to use. I may mention that the same potatoes were part of the enticing ad. which had offered me 'first class cuisine in refined, secluded neighbourhood'. I was not a day in residence till I realised I had been taken to the bosom of a crowd of the most agonatastical gurriers I ever came across.

'Do you not realise, young men,' said Mrs Paw-Nay, 'dat the best part of a pom, or poe-tato, lies nearest the shkin?'

I looked around when I heard her addressing my Solitary Eminence as 'men' but could see no bystanders. I was in no mood for pleasantries, as I had already consumed the *biftek* Madam had served and had a distinct feeling of dog in the manger. (Pardon, dog in the *mangeur*, I meant.) Besides, I spoke the language.

'I don't know anny such a ting,' I retorted. 'Th'oney gud ting next the skin I ever heerd of,' says I, 'is red flanngel. What's so gud undher the skin of a spud?'

'There's salts,' says Mrs Paw-Nay, 'an' there's . . .'

'An there's what?' says I.

'There's iron . . . an' there's phoosphoroos, an' there's protyins.'

I told her that if that was true, I'd get it all back in the morning rasher, because it was knuwn, I said, and well-knuwn that she got six-and-six a week for household slops (*dîner* to me) from an arch-gurrier that kep' two secret pigs in a disused lavvyterry in the concrete yard at the back of the house he shared with 102 other persons. She did not like this at all and flounced towards the door, saying: 'I never like to see gud noorishment thrun away, young men. I know what yer goin' to get when yer a bit older.'

'What?' I barked. I knew the reply would be good by the way she had the door poised for an exit slam.

'A speenal deforminty!' *Slam!*

*   *   *

Many people behave like Mrs Paw-Nay, though in a different sphere. They impatiently skip the pages of Small Ads in the newspapers, quite unaware that they are the best part of the paper – mankind's market place, forum of opportunity, haven of joy, mausoleum of quaint hopes. Recently I read a very good Small Ad. With sorrow I confess it was not in the *Irish Times* (*Eire*), O.B.E. it appeared, but in the columns of our sprightly junior contemporary, the *Co. Dublin Evening Mail*, *H. Dip. in Ed.* I quote:

A person writing book would like to hear from another with knowledge of same and having a typewriter. Box . . .

I read that again. Then I laid down the paper and fell into deepest reverie. The ash dropped inanely from my cigar. I became splayed so awkwardly with my deep thoughts in my deep chair in Santry Great Hall that you would swear that I suffered from a speenal deforminty.

*   *   *

What class of man, I wondered, could have put in so lonely, so exquisite a Small Ad? Could it be that as he scrawled it out in night's lateness with rusty pen, he was seated in a tiny whitewashed bedroom with plywood walls in a refined, secluded district? Heavens, I could see Mrs Paw-Nay, candle in hand, quietly opening the door.

'I suooppose you are aware, young men, that la loomy hair electreek is most costly?'

'Oi am writhing a buk.' Sullen tone.

'La, la! There are four of thim dawn the shtairs, thin. Would ye nawt be bitter aff in bid? Or can ye nawt woo Dame Shlumber now?'

'Oi'm writhing a buk.' Dejection.

'What ye want is more veetemeens an' a gud doze of Galaaabyur Salts, young men.'

*   *   *

I lacked the courage to (or possessed the sense not to) answer that Small Ad. That way lay shattering disappointment. No man could live up to such an ad. But man, whoever thou art, I wish thee luck.

> What leaf-fringed legent haunts about thy
> >   shape
> Of deities or mortals, or of both,
> In Kickham Road or Dartry?
> What men or gods are these?
> >   What maidens loath?
> What mad pursuit? What struggle to escape?
> What pipes and timbrels? What wild ecstasy?

I can only hope devoutly that the book was written and that the author met that person he sought so dearly, another with knowledge of same.

The Paw-Nay Injun

A few recent recollections of mine of the days when I was in digs in Rathmines *chez* Mrs Paw-Nay remind me that I have told nothing of her remarkable husband. (I need hardly say that her real name was not 'Paw-Nay'; that was the sound she made every time she was searching for her glasses, which had a habit of escaping from the black ribbon by which she had them anchored to her immense bosom.)

It is very difficult to describe Mr Paw-Nay. One can say that he wore a bowler hat, that his red, round face had red-rimmed eyes, or that the bulge in his tightish trousers revealed that he suffered from piano-leg. Such facts don't

seem to convey the immensity of his personality. From his
bulb-nose there appeared to hang an immense khaki moustache resembling in disarray those sinister fungoid draperies
often pictured as ornamenting great trees in the steaming,
upper reaches of the Amazon.

He came in silently to find me sitting at the kitchen
range or, as Mrs Paw-Nay called it 'my far-from-defeesent
gree de queezeen'. It was our first meeting. Mr Paw-Nay did
not show any surprise. He gave me a glance of mild hostility,
as if I was an envelope from the Coimisinéirí Ioncaim. He
flopped in a chair and sighed.

'Where is the grandma?' he asked.

I presumed he meant his wife, and said she was out. He
sighed again.

* * *

'I believe ya,' he said. 'The time I come back from Indya
destroyded with malyaaria and marchured with Indyin hives,
the grandma was out too. If ya seen me tryin' to make meself
a *smahan* of beef tea in a skillet with a handle on it that was
bruk, ye'd say a prayer for me on yer bended knees.'

'She had left no supper for you?'

'Not even a hard *turteen* nor a *juck-in-durish* of *blawhach*.
'Course, I was away five year.'

'Oh!'

'In Indya. And she wasn't out at all, I needn't tell ya. I
come on her when I gun upstairs, rowled and double-
rowlded inside in the bed.'

'She wasn't ill, wash she?'

'Parlatic.'

'Really?'

'That wumman . . . that wumman had a firkin of stilumants in her craw – *ishka bey*, brillianteen mixed with
brandy-wine, and lumps of *cawka milish* soaked in sherry
gargle. A great wumman, the grandma. When I got into the
bed she half-wuk and says to me: 'Are y'all right, George?'

'Well, better a late welcome than none.'

'Ah, yes. Sairtintly. 'Course me name's *Meehawl* – ya
knew that? *George* – ah?'

'Well, well . . .'

'Couldn't sleep atchall. I was lain there for hours,

mooskeeta-net an' all over me, but th'Indyin hives was somethin' cruel. At the heel of the hunt I gev meself a dose of moorphya that I got off a hop-off-me-thumb of a lascar guttie in Poart Sad, powerful stuff. Some of the crowd say it makes you think yer in an aeroplane but do you know what I'm goina-tellya? It makes ya think ya *ARE* an aeroplane.'

'How many engines?'

'Four, an' about a hundred purpellors workin' out of them.'

* * *

'Tell me this much,' Mr Paw-Nay said after a pause. 'Are ya *sairtin* the grandma's out?'

Here I unbent a bit and said: 'I seen the hat, and I seen the grapes.'

'She never wears grapes,' Mr Paw-Nay said sharply. That's plums she wears. But *iss kumma. Naw bocklesh.* But she had a right to be here and me oney back from Indya. D'ya know? If it was oney to make me a skillet of *brahawn* for me tea. I think . . . I think I'll hop into the bed above . . .'

To prove the honesty of his intention, he got up, gave me a military salute, and carefully put on his heavy stained overcoat. Then he left without a word, softly closing the door.

That record of my first meeting with Mr Paw-Nay may seem pointless and banal. In the event, it was most impressive. The dignity of his departure is incommunicable. It was in terms of Milton I sat there remembering him:

> But his face
> Deep scars of thunder had intrencht, and care
> Sat on his faded cheek, but under brows
> Of dauntless courage, and considerate pride
> Waiting revenge . . .

I decided to go to bed, too: it was obvious that Mrs Paw-Nay was dining at the French Embassy that night, and that her advent in enflunkeyed *voiture* would be of the order of 3 a.m. So I went to bed. But first I took off my overcoat.

Things Said in my Ear Ring

BAAAAAH!

This verbal explosion occurred just as a carefully refolded copy of the *Irish Times* was slammed on a mahogany counter matured by about a century of slopped drinks. The speaker of that BAAAAAH, whom we will call The Angry Man, had addressed it to another person whom we will call The Man Who Knows Everything and Everybody And Knows What Goes On. That boils down to the unlikely and unpronounceable total of TMWKEAEAKWGO.

This representative of the Tmwkeaeakwgo class was perfectly in order. When he got the BAAAAAH blast with the preceding slap of the newspaper on the counter, he did not betray perturbation and was unhurried in the job of disengaging his moustached countenance from the boglike surface of a new pint while his eyes, assisted by two pairs of spectacles, continued to stare at the *Manchester Guardian*. The glance he finally conferred revealed that he was a total (if not exactly a teetotal) stranger. It also conveyed to me, some yards away, a message such as 'Pray continue, friend, I will help you gladly if I can.'

The conversation now following then occurred, and I present it as faithfully as I can, presenting the remarks of The Angry Man in italics. The answers of Tmwkeaeakwgo are in ordinary type.

*　　*　　*

This rag! And this Myles Magoplin! What is the meaning of that muck? What is he driving at? I am not going to stand for attacks on the Catlic Church. Who is this Myles na Scaplogue? The what? I don't know what you're talking about.

I did not open my mouth for any purpose to be associated with articulation. You appear to be in search of information. It is best to take questions singly. That procedure simplifies the supply of information. I do not personally know what annoys you concerning matter appearing under the signature of Myles na Gopaleen but I will ask you a question which is – to employ a witticism – a rather Irish way of answering a question. Do you know Myles na Gopaleen?

I sertaintly do not know Myles no Gáoplance and if I seen him I would report it to the Guards.

He is not the sort of person you imagine him to be. As a matter of fact he is not only a gentleman but a decent man as well.

I see. What sort of a man is this Myles na Scapulars when he is at home?

A tall man with glasses. He happens to be a personal friend of mine and actually comes in here occasionally. A tall man with glasses, elderly, and a bit on the austere side. He is of a retiring nature, if that is the correct phrase, his drink is a small sherry and he will instantly leave any place wherein loose language is employed. But there is another thing about him which I will mention only in confidence.

What else can you say about this saint?

Hardly a word appearing under his pseudonym in the *Irish Times* is written by himself. To use a witticism, every dog and divil in the country writes it, or wants to be let write it, and it is no secret that certain high-up men write it now and again. For example, the head man in charge of Maynooth was supposed to be a regular contributor.

I am beginning to have my suspicions about you, my bucko. You are a friend of Myles Mickoplick, the tall man with the glasses. I'm away.

Good morning.

What was that?

GOOD MORNING!

Right. I thought you said something else.

The True Guide

The ensuing dialogue occurs between a true Dubalin Maan and a countryman who 'knows' Dublin and wishes to come to settle in the city. The Dubalin Maan is 'marking the card' of the latter. The countryman's responses are in italic type.

Mean to say, the idea is that the next time there's an All-Ireland Final, I'll get a cheap ticket up, and STAY.

Do you know Dubalin at all, apart from Wynn's Hotel?

Well . . . I suppose I do.

Do you know where the O'Connell Momunent is?

The what?

The Momunent. Listen, do you know Keogh's of Bachelor's Walk?

'Course I do.

Come out on to the kay, wheel to yer left, walk a hunderd yards, and you are at the Momunent. Do you understand me?

Certaintly.

Right. Now supposing you want to see the new bus station put up be Mickey Scott. Walk down the kay past the Corinthinian cinema and ask any guard to direct you to John Keating's of Store Street. John is a very decent skin. He'll give you all the instructions about how to get to the bus station and a damn fine get-up it is by the same token. Now suppose you want to get to the City Hall, though I don't know what you'd want to go there for because there's damn-all in it oney pitchers of kings and oul fellas. Make yer way to McCabe's of Dame Street and you're there. Did you ever hear of the Halfpenny Bridge?

No.

It's just facing Murray's of the Kay.

You mentioned Dan O'Connell's Momunent. Isn't there a ruined tower at his grave in Glasnevin? How would I get there at all?

Are you serious, man? You go past Matt Hedigan's at the Brian Boru House. Dean's Grange, of course, is near Baker's.

They tell me this Theatre Royal is a very big joint, the third biggest in the whole world. Supposin' the Dixie Minstrels was on and I wanted to get there. Where IS the place?

That's easy. It's near two places – Phil O'Reilly's of Hawkins's Street and Mulligan's of Poolbeg Street. Do you folly me?

* * *

Supposin' the married sister was sendin' up a few bastes be lurry. Where's the Cattle Market?

It's part and parcel of the City Arms Hotel, for goodness sake. Above in Proosia Street.

It's a great town, there's no doubt. Gob I think I'll come and

*get a house in a place they call Ballyfermot. Five bob a week,
I believe. The way it is, I was thinkin' it was time meself and
Annie fixed things up. I'm nearly fifty. Know what I mean?*

Take your time now, but I'll tell you this much. Know
Mooney's of Parnell Street?

I don't think I do.

Dammit, Parnell's arm is pointing at it. In any case the
Rotunda Hospital is right opposite.

Thanks.

There's a great show of horses and bastes every year at
the R.D.S. in Ballsbridge, a real fancy place where you'll pay
four and tuppence for a glass of malt and like it. Know where
that place is?

I certainly do not.

Opposite Martin Crowes's.

*Do you know this chiner Briscoe at all. They tell me he is one
of the best and marked out as a future Tear Shark. He is
supposed to live in a place they call the Mansion House. Where
is the Mansion House?*

Know the Dawson Lunge?

I don't, and I never go into them lounges.

That's a very high-class lunge, full of doctors, insurance
fellas, bookies, and tell you who you might meet there.

Who is that?

Myles Ma Goplin howareye!

Lord save us!

In any case the Mansion House is opposite the Dawson
Lunge. Let me know if you think of gettin' up to live here.
Cheers!

Cheers.

Seen and Sawn

Before the news here is a police message. I invited people to
write to me, and one has, from the county of Mayo. (Stop
that 'God help us!' plaint in the background!) He said he
was suffering from a severe attack of Bangor Erris Sipelas.
I told this correspondent that there was nothing for it only
five hundred million Oxford units of pencillin.

He ordered the consignment, and it came in the next day by the B. & I., marked FRAGILE and endored.

Is it old age or sentimentimentality? Never mind that last word – the typewriter keeps on commenting, and can now and again invent a beautiful and unextinguishable word like 'endored'. I leave it. I dare not touch this sort of thing. I can think only of Shakespeare's sonnet 'Shall I Compare Thee To a Summer's Day?'

In face of such competition, one does not dispute.

* * *

The police message over, I now come to what I meant to talk about. I was being entertained in a house (of all places) the other evening when I heard the lady of the house mentally chastising her son of twelve, or so. He had said something like *I seen George today.*

He was told this: 'Don't let me hear you saying "seen" again. The word is SAW.'

I nearly cried when I heard the enunciation of this appalling heresy. The notion that SEEN is an illiterate alternative for SAW is so mistaken that I can think of no printable terms of rebuke.

They are, of course, entirely different words; more, their occasions are indeed different.

* * *

'He was run out of a pub in Ballaghadereen at the closing hour. Do you know what I mean? In any case he thought he would like another drink. So he attacked another pub that was closed, and gun in through the winda . . .'

Here the recitalist makes an enormous ceremony about lighting his pipe. Ultimately, out comes the concluding remark for which all present are holding patiently on:

'*I seen him myself. I seen him all right.*'

I leave it to anybody who understands the use of words to substitute the word SAW for SEEN in that context, and see (or should I say *saw?*) what you get.

* * *

I have myself sawn a few conversations of this kind. The word SEEN, has, in fact, a faintly theological air, and is generally accepted in this country as *proof* of some unlikely proposition.

Fairies? Of course there are fairies. I seen them. And I seen the well they went down. Fairies?

* * *

Perhaps the most important branch of this mythology concerns the Irish gentleman who persists in seeing himself, mostly in the midst of ludicrous and unrewarding transactions. None has yet told me of the circumstances in which he saw himself. 'I seen meself marching into Leopardstown Park as sober as a judge and handing over eight fivers to a man that was standing up, *against* ——. Oh, I needn't tell you, I should have me head examined . . .'

FOOTNOTE: I have just read what I have written, and I know that it does not treat its enormous subject adequately. But should one nowadays call that lovely sonnet of Shakespeare 'Shall Ike Compare to a Summer's Day?'

Well, all right, I seen you coming, reader!

This Day

Dear Reader! (Don't be fooled by this form of address because we fellows who write for the papers absolutely loathe readers. They are all intent on proving that they are smarter than myself!) And they nearly prove it!

I had better repeat that word. *Nearly*.

* * *

I wanted to tell my dear readers that they are not this morning reading the article they think they are. This is a new, last-moment script. I spent two days writing the other one. Having typed it, I read it. The suppressed editor in me instantly said NO. It was very learned but ALL WRONG. It aimed at the heart of childhood. Its foul barb was aimed even at myself as I was forty years ago – a dirty small boy. (Do you believe it? I personally treat the theory with great doubt.)

* * *

This suppressed article was entitled 'December 24th'. As I have said, it was learned. It *proved* that this day is not Christmas Eve. Its composition was interrupted nine times by carol singers. My horribly keen mind noted that five out of the nine groups sang the same carol. I still went on reading one of the lives of Martin Luther in German. I still wanted to make my rotten point that today is not Christmas Eve, that Our Lord was not born on Christmas Day, and that all that crowd who have, even already, sent me cards, are quite mistaken.

How right I am in the sphere of fact! And now wrong in the far more important sphere of what one feels. Christmas *is* Christmas, and that's all about it.

* * *

I hope to publish this article, possibly in July. Notwithstanding all the labour and erudition that went to its making, it is astonishingly easy to establish the theory that Christmas never happened and does not exist. The paraphernalia that traditionally surrounds the Event is quite impossible. Snow never falls in Bethlehem in December, the robin is quite unknown there, and the evergreen holly, which can flourish anywhere, is unknown in that part of the world. I am in great danger of publishing the meat of the article I have written and suppressed. I will be honest and finally confess that crackers, plum pudding and whiskey are as well known in Bethlehem as they are here.

* * *

The fact is that I like Christmas. There was a time when everybody in search of intellectual eminence could attain the same by denouncing the feast. Some people actually did so. Bernard Shaw made a preliminary name for himself by denouncing Shakespeare, and later made sure of fame by assailing Christmas as an obscene mercantile rite. His hero, Ibsen, did the same thing. Longfellow disliked Christmas. Even the great Beethoven has told of his dislike for December 25th. I, bigger boy than any of them (in my own estimation), nearly said the same thing.

I didn't however.

I now content myself by wishing YOU a happy Christmas.

I know it's old-fashioned stuff. I know nothing wrong with old-fashioned stuff.

Bad Humour

Attendance at a funeral recently brought me to a district which I know and wherein I am known, and I thought I would renew acquaintance with a pub run by a gentleman known as the Boss, with the assistance of his nephew Christy. I found the Boss alone, glaring morosely at a newspaper spread on the counter. And the following was the conversation:

The hard man! Good morning, I said.

Japers! Yerself? Well, by gor. You'll have the usual? Right, I suppose you were above at the funeral. Dacent poor oul skin, divilabetter. I seen that maan goin' home a Christmas Eve with a gold clock for th'oul wan and he didn't get that for matches – he ped for it and ped well for it, I'll go bail he ped a fiver. And there was luvly choimes in it, he had it goin' here on the counter, it would be grand for the drawn room.

Yes. I agree. Where's Christy?

The nephya? He's doin' nuthin' at all oney flyin' in the face of Providence, he won't fill up the form.

What form?

The compensation form. He says he'll play a waitin' game because he knows the compensation is goin' to be riz up. I warned and I double-warnded that thooleramawn of an ownshucck that he'll get nuthin' at all at the heel of the hunt, and me here wore out with no help nor peace. Lord save us he has me near druv to this traction.

Was he in an accident?

Was he WHAT? Did you not hear? He banjaxed the humorist. I thought that was well known.

He what?

Listen. The time we had the snow, word come down wan night that some unfortunate oul wan gev herself a toss up the hill there beyant and was lying out there in the snow with a sprainded anakle. So course me bould Christy could do anything bar mind his own business, what right had an oul wan to be up there in that class of weather at all, I'd lave her there. But course Christy, that has the nose near wore off him pokin' it into what doesn't condsarn him achall, puts on the coat and out with him – *and a glass of MY brandy in his pocket, ah? AH?* The rescue brigade, faith of our fathers and how are ye!

Well what happened?

Tell you what happened, me bould son. He don't come back achall, that's what happened. How do I know, says I to meself, that's it's an oul wan up the hill, maybe it's a young wan. Do you folly me, ah? So when closin' time cem, I took a dander up meself, would you blame me? What do I find oney me hard Christy lying on the side of the road lettin' unmerciful roars out of him. Me showlder, says he, me SHOWLDER! He was after givin' himself the divil of a toss aaalthegither and he couldn't get up, he was like a man parlatic aSaherda night. When I got him up I nearly had to carry him home, he was like a sag of potatoes. Imagine a man of my age carryin' a nephya home on me back!

You are still a fine figure of a man.

And if you heard the whingin' and moanin' and cursin' and prayin' and cryin' out for the priest and the doctor. I never seen the like of it nor won't. More betoken, we got the doctor and after he has a good luck at me brave nephya, he turns to me and says: 'He has bruk the humorist.' It would take three months, maybe more, to get the humorist fixed, says he. And what am I supposed to do, says I, mean to say I'm to run the damn shop ON ME OWN. Certaintly, says he, because do you know what I'm going to tell you, that maaan . . . that maaan won't pull pints nor open a bottle of stout for a long time, he must get pairfict rest, says he, in bed, says he, and yez musn't excite him in anny way. *We musn't excite the nephya, ah?* I'm goin' to tell you that class of talk was excitin' ME, crippled with corns all me life and mister-me-friend this doc standin' there as bould as brazen brass tellin' me I can spend sixteen hours a day behind this counter wearin' the croobs off me down to the shanks, thanks very much, but one thing I must not do is excite the darlint nephya, did you ever hear the like of it since the day you were born?

No.

Ah but listen. The doc asks me does Christy live here. Be dad he does not, says I, he's in digs with an oul crawhen

up the road that has bad eye disease. Well, says he, this
maaan must get proper noorishment and care, and he asks
me to get him an egg and a fork. I do that. Now, says he,
get me a glass of brandy. AH? *Brandy!* When he has the
egg bet up in the brandy, he hands the glass to the nephya.
Now, says he, swally that, me good maaan, it won't do you
a bit of harm. *It won't do you a bit of harm!* Then he tells me
to get a cair and have Christy druv home, that he'll see him
tamorra . . . and away with him, lavin' me alone with the
nephya, holdin' his humorist that was gettin' swoll up
good-o and an empty glass of MY brandy. Don't talk to me
about communasm.

But Christy was probably in great pain.

I don't give a damn if he broke his two humorists, the
squirt. And the yarns I heard about him afterwards from
the lads, propped up in bed with pillas and cooshins, *gettin'
fed* be oul Mrs Thingumbob like a baby, can't do anthin'
for himself, melia murdher if these wasn't a bottle of stout
with his dinner and an egg for his tea, lyin' all day there
readin' d'Irish Press and smokin' any God's amount of
cigarettes. Oh the life of Reilly there's no doubt.

*What happened the poor old lady Christy went out to
rescue?*

Her? Never heard another word about her.

The Nephya

Recently I had an opportunity of revisiting the little country
pub where, as I have related, the Boss had told me how his
nephew and assistant Christy had fractured his left humerus
in a fall. I had intended to inquire about Christy's progress
and have a few drinks while also absorbing what was bound
to be extended exegesis. I was astonished to find Christy
himself alone behind the counter, thoughtfully examining
his knuckles and scowling to himself.

How the hell are ya? he said.

Very well. I thought your humerus——

Me humorist is bruk. It's not just fractured, mind. It's
BRUK. I come a terrible fall on it. Nobody'll ever know

what I went through with that humorist, it was like bein' in purgatory. The landlady I have, of course, is a grend oul scout, divilabetter, a very dirty woman I need hairdly say but a heart of the purest gold. If it wasn't for the brandy an' raw eggs she gev me, forbye a raw egg for me tea, declare to goodness I'd be a dead man now.

But you're working?

What else could I do? We'd put the licence in danger if we closed up, and that wouldn't do at all. Mean to say, there's some limit.

* * *

But where's the Boss?

The . . . the . . . BOSS?

Here a low sound, starting off in the boots growing in volume, with cacophonous undulation and emerging as a 'laugh' from a grotesquely distorted gob.

Yes, the Boss.

Shure the Boss is banjaxed. Here's a nice bottle of stout for you. He's gone to the wall. Good enough for the oul cod, too. Too good for him. He was never done looking for pity for himself and his corns and his boonyins. By gob he knows now what rale suffering is, he knows now what I went through an' never a word of complaint passed me lips, nor wouldn't.

Don't tell me he has broken his humorist too?

Notataaal. Wait'll I tell ya. Wait till you hear this wan. This'll make you laugh. He come up every now and again to the digs to see how I was muryaa, if the humorist was bruk altogether standin' in a dish on the table in me room, do you know what he'd say? 'You must be gettin' better,' he'd say, 'if you can have a joint like that for your dinner.' Just spyin' on me. He'd always bring a baby Power full of brandy wine. Know what that is? Nothin' oney red biddy. Would you like to try a drop of it? Pysin. Take the paint off a back door.

No thanks. What happened?

* * *

Says I to him wan day I was propped up in bed with cooshins: 'You're not looking well at all, do you know that?' 'What other way would I look,' says he, 'doin' three men's work below in the shop, and the corns so bad that I do be in slippers?' The cheek of that! Man that never done a day's work in his life, nor won't. He was a queer colour do you know, half white and half yalla. He looked like a heathen Chinee.

We all look like that now and again.

Ah no, not like he did. The doc was here lookin' at me humorist the next time the Boss come. Declare to me godfathers the face would frighten you. It's not like a Chinee he looked but like a red man out of Indya. The eyes was poppin' out of him. The doc seen and was starin'. 'Listen here me good maaan,' says he, 'take off your coat and lie down on that couch till we have a screw at you.' 'Sairtintly,' says the Boss, very annoyed, 'an' I hope ya'll find me humorist is gone too, because that man in the bed is drunk,' says he, 'an' it can't be the worst thing could happen you in this valley of tears be all accounts.' Wasn't that a dirty wan, th'oul bags?

* * *

What did the doctor say?

He straightens up after a while an' says he: 'Do you know what YOU have? You have a very bad dose,' says he, 'of the yalla jaunders.' 'Is that a fact,' says the Boss, very sarcastic. 'Well now isn't that a very strange ting. Would you mind tellin' me what is the yalla jaunders?'

And what was it, pray?

'There's something wrong with your boil,' says the doc, 'an' it's very sairyus. Ya'll have to go to bed mediately an' for your life don't eat anny fat, it's pysin to a man in your situation,' saays he. Well luckit. The Boss very near collapsded. He mutters about the shop and who's going to mind it. 'That man in the bed with the bad humorist,' he says, 'I'll put another coupla yards of stickin' plaster on him and then I think he'll be strong enough to mind the pub.' Caana you beat that? ME! Hah? A man with his poor bones all bruk up. Did you ever in your life hear of such hairtless crulety?

Never. What happened?

The usual of course. Joe Soap gets the works. Some of that crowd would take you out of your coffin if they were hard up would take fourth at solo. A right crowd. Up I had to get as wake as a kitten, get into me clothes, with the doc helpin' me, an' an old tie to keep the trousers up because you couldn't put braces over the humorist. The Boss is druv home to bed be the doc an' to get needles stuck in him. Me, I start feedin' beer to the corner boys that lives around these parts. Isn't that good? Hah? There's life for you if you like, there's no livin' doubt.

There is not indeed.

I suppose you'll have a small wan for the road.

I suppose so.

G'luck!

G'luck!

Night Must Fall

Night must fall. Ever hear those three words before? They spell out the name of a bad novel, a poor play and a rotten film. Why was this piece of bad work so successful? Because people liked the title.

The corollary to this disclosure is admittedly fairly horrible. All you have to do is think of a good title; leave the writing to somebody else or just get the pages full of any sort of print to take the naked look off them. Nobody is going to read your novel. Have a good title and your fortune is made.

People all over the world expect bestsellers. They are as essential as new waistlines for women, new cars, new opening hours for pubs. How are other people aware you are not dead unless you know about the changes, unless you are fully informed on the new stuff? The expected thing must happen. Otherwise there is no point in expecting anything, and very little justification for being alive at all. *Night must fall.* But supposing tomorrow did not dawn? Suppose water did not come from the tap? Suppose the policeman, instead of answering your mannerly inquiry about where a street was, struck you with his fist? Suppose – to push the thing a bit far – night did not fall?

* * *

This philosophical exordium arises from a feeling on my part of neglect. My house in Santry has not been raided.

No hooded wagons full of able-bodied young fellows have pulled up outside that door, no revolvers have been discharged in the air, that housekeeper of mine has not been taken away in tears. Why is that? Do they think I am no longer a revolutionary?

In some State jobs in this country you are not eligible for appointment unless you can speak Irish or are over six feet tall or are a niece of a Cabinet Minister. (Don't be troubled about your sex if you are a male and still want to be the niece of a Cabinet Minister, the thing can be fixed.)

I am entirely in agreement with any arrangement ordaining that the Six and the Twenty-six Counties should be overtly police states. I ask only for a bit of warning and an opportunity to get into the police. The right to arrest the civilian population and hold them without trial must be jealously safeguarded. It is an essential part of the whole apparatus of civilisation and decency. The only detail in this scheme not already minutely attended to is simply that a few of us are still not Cabinet Ministers, nieces thereof, policemen, nor even members of the Free State Army. What is the world coming to at all. Declare to the godfathers, I met a chap last Friday who was thirty-four if he was a day who swore to me he hadn't a pension. See what I mean? Discrimination.

Speaking Literally

How many kinds of books are there? Let us say the read, the read and forgotten, the unread, *and the unwritten*. That last class is most important.

If I mention *Confessions of an English Opium Eater*, one hears the murmur, 'Ah, De Quincéy.' Yes, but what else did he write? His complete works were published in America over a century ago, and they filled twenty volumes. I wish I could read them but they are not to be had. (There you have still another category.) De Quincéy, born of a settled family in Manchester, had a hand-to-mouth education, so to speak, but nothing would do him at the age of seventeen only (1) to be able to speak Greek fluently and, (2) to run away from home to immerse himself in nameless London squalors and agonies.

He was an excellent writer, having, above all other symptoms of mastery in literature – discursiveness: and irony, unobtrusive, as it always should be. See the deliberately funny gravity in this description of a queer character:

He breakfasted alone: indeed, his tea equipage would hardly have admitted of his hazarding an invitation to a second person – any more than the quantity of esculent *matériel*, which, for the most part, was little more than a roll, or a few buscuits . . .

Who but a master could think of 'esculent *matériel*' as the right way of saying 'food'?

* * *

Is there any point at all in writing unless the writer is *certain* that many people will read the words, submit to their alchemy? I have asked an actor whether a company could go through a serious play (in no rehearsal sense) without a soul in the auditorium. He said NO; the audience is part of the play, a ship is useless without water setra setra setra.

Then why did Joe Holloway write fifteen million words about Abbey Theatre first nights? I like to think it was in the hope that he might manage to get half a million published (ten volumes called *Abbey First Nights* with the magnificent sub-title *A Fragment*).

Joe, remember, was the architect of the Dolphin Hotel, which, when a-building, he refused to inspect by going up ladders. He examined the work through spy-glasses from the upper windows of a tall building opposite. That class of man isn't made any more.

* * *

Let me talk about another thing which has been much on my mind for many years. I got a slap of it last week, the slap of a flat fish in the face. There is in Kerry a young school teacher named Bryan MacMahon who . . . writes. He started an article in a contemporary last week as follows:

This week I confess myself tempted by a variety of topics: (*a*) The Cow of Clare (*b*) The All-Ireland Football Final (*c*) Listowel Races (*d*) Kinsale and (*e*) pratie-coornanes, skidderie-wadderies, shellaky-bookles and pooka-pyles.

I read that in bed *before* breakfast. I could nearly hear the spotless and ornate eiderdown murmur 'Good man yerself, thanks.'

I don't blame the young teacher, for he has been taught. The problem is to find out who really started this thing. I fancy it was Carleton, and that he did it quite unwittingly. His was an age of terrible despond, poverty, illiteracy and violence, and his portraits of the peasantry were sincere; people actually spoke as he said they did. He was a very good writer by any standard. Others such as Lover, Somerville and Ross, may be said to be perverted Carletons, showing the natives and their ways in a canon of amiable cawboguery; they were perhaps the founders of the 'school' which can in 1954 present the nosegay of pratie-coornanes, skidderie-wadderies, shellaky-bookles and pooka-pyles.

* * *

Perhaps the next isolated phase was that of Synge–George Moore–Gregory–Martyn, with Yeats in the background. They persisted in the belief that poverty and savage existence on remote rocks was a most poetical way for people to be, provided they were other people.

Of that bunch, the worst was Synge. Here we had a moneyed dilettante coming straight from Paris to study the peasants of Aran not knowing a syllable of their language, then coming back to pour forth a deluge of homemade jargon all over the Abbey stage and on top of the head of the young Dr Larchet at the piano. Noggins of porter, the white boards, the long nights after Samhain, surely. The irony of it!

When in the West, Synge considered himself (read his own account) an accomplished *savant* and artist examining primitive communities and penetrating to their hearts through the crucible of poesy, but making sure to wear a strong bodycoat against the chill winds when engaged at his sacred tasks out of doors: whereas he was an ignorant affected interloper in a uniquely decent, stable and civilised community.

While this was going on Lady Gregory (whom I can never mentally quite dissociate from Queen Victoria) was, so to speak, quietly knitting her Kiltartan, as well as being the Maeceness to Yeats.

* * *

Many and many have laboured in this poisoned vineyard. I attempt no ill word against the dead, but the most recent and most spectacular performer was Aodh de Blacam. He invented a fabulous world of whangs (leather boot-laces), boxty, poundies, crubeens, sheelamagoorlas, fairy mounds, crassogues, patterns, the Mountains of Mourne, *mo phíopa goirid donn* – a frightening apparatus.

Not to be left out of the picture are Sean O'Faoláin and Frank O'Connor, with stories about wee Annie going to her first confession, stuff about country funerals, old men in chimney nooks after fifty years in America, will-making, match-making – just one long blush for many an innocent man like me, who never harmed them.

* * *

The set-up is this. These people turn angrily on the British and roar: 'How dare you insult us with your stage Irishman, a monkey-faced leering scoundrel in ragged knee-breeches and a tail coat, always drunk and threatening anybody in sight with his shillelagh? We can put together a far better stage Irishman ourselves, thank you. The Irish Stage Irishman is the best in the world.'

I have done – temporarily. A vanatee, agraw, would ye put out me supper like a colleen dhas, a bowl of stirabout med with injun meal and a noggin of buttermilk, surely?

Memento Mori

I have been reading – admittedly in a small thesaurus titled *Queer Facts* – this undoubtedly queerish item: 'Brookwood Cemetery, in Surrey, is the only cemetery in the world to have two fully licensed bars!'

I tried to check, first, was there any such place as Brookwood, in Surrey, and regret to report that there is no record of it in the archives of my house in Santry. It may, of course, be a very small place, and I am by no means traversing the truth of the item I have quoted.

The main thing that astonishes me is not that there should be facilities for drinking in a cemetery, but that there should be TWO bars. Why not just one big one – or is the cemetery so vast that two must be provided to avoid long walks?

On consideration, I see nothing particularly inappropriate in having bars in a cemetery, particularly if it is in a remote country district. A cemetery is a place of public concourse, and there is no reason why human needs should not be attended to. Why is there no toilet accommodation in, say, Deansgrange, which is a very big place?

* * *

In the great sarcophagi disinterred in Egypt and elsewhere it was found to be a commonplace of ancient civilisation that the chamber containing the body of a dead king had also his weapons and a supply of food and drink. There may be some atavistic echo of that concept in the bars of Brookwood Cemetery. It could be brought to a firmer stage if a pipe were installed leading from the surface to the interior of the coffin.

I can almost hear some simple-minded reader ask how a corpse could let the crowd in the bar know that he wanted a drink? Silly question. By tapping on the inner lid of the coffin, of course, *and using the Mors code*.

* * *

Seriously, though, what is our genuine attitude to death? Primitive peoples found death occurring otherwise than from violence – wounds in battle or accidentally falling over a precipice – as quite inexplicable. Death from natural causes they attributed to magic and sorcery, and it was this belief that gave witch-doctors their immense power.

We, as Christians, know better. From whatever cause, the immortal soul leaves the body and the latter is venerated as having been the temporary temple of that soul; it is devoutly interred in consecrated ground. Relatives are grief-stricken but it is the grief of separation not despair. Indeed, the attitude in some quarters has been: there is a good man his job done, and gone home. Death in rural Ireland has many a time been made the subject of something little short of jubilation, and staider townspeople have often been shocked by what appeared to them to be unseemly levity and in-sobriety at wakes. Again, what is to be inferred from the fact that nearly all country graveyards here are in an unbelievable state of ruin and neglect, sometimes with the bones of the dead kicking about in the tangle of weeds, thistles, brambles and collapsed headstones? I can't readily answer that.

I mentioned Deansgrange.

> Sceptre and crown
> Will tumble down
> And in the clay be equal made
> With the poor crooked scythe and spade.

That is very far from true at Deansgrange, a pretty formidable necropolis. There is the strictest segregation of classes. Any visitor will be deeply shocked by the unbelievable vulgarity and ostentation of some of the monuments to the opulent. Some are openly pagan, and it seems that relatives can erect absolutely anything they like. *Sunt lacrimae rerum et mentem mortalia tangunt.*

Pagust

The Post Office – at least the Irish one – is surely the strangest of imaginable organisms. This fact was borne in upon me – but not for the first time – a few days ago when I asked in a sub-office for a threepenny stamp. I was handed a twopenny and a penny stamp. I said I wanted a THREE-PENNY stamp, as in fact I did because the letter was for a foreigner interested in stamps.

'We're outa da thrippennies,' the elderly dame said. 'Ya'll hafta try da G.P.O. or somewheres.' Here was a pathetic vision of a poor little huckster being walked on by a bully of a giant wholesaler. 'You'll get your thruppennies just when it suits us to give them, and if you don't shut up you'll get none.'

Another time in another office I asked civilly for a Wireless Receiving Licence. Preposterous and meaningless as the term is, it is the official term and I used it. The presiding fat oul wan – a true member of the class I dub *femme de siècle* – snapped.

'First wan or renewyil?'

I merely repeated my request (or demand) in accordance with law.

'Didya hear me? *Is it renewyil?*'

This battle with Arrah na Posts proceeded to the point when I was forced to ask her in courtly English whether I was to take it that she was refusing me a licence. She then ignored me but said to a companion postess: 'Da cheek a some peeepil!' So I am without a licence and thus has my radio been bastardised. But I play fair. I never listen to it.

*　　*　　*

I do not disguise that some of these collisions can be entertaining and, heaven forgive me, I have occasionally sought them. Once I strolled into a sub-office and said to the immense stampeuse that a cadoonas gyer chastied from me. She stared at me:

'Whaaa? The who?'

When I repeated the request, she turned and bellowed into the interior: 'Teresa! Come up here outa that. There's an Oirishman here!' And when Teresa appeared, I saw she was young and quite attractive. I raised my hat and said:

'Chascheen cadoonas gyer wooim.'

She smiled dazzlingly and said:

'Shaa.'

But she still stood there. When I repeated the request, she again very pleasantly said 'Shaa' but did not budge. It was a moment of crisis but I was not defeated. I got down on my hunkers, waved my hands paw-like and cried 'Woof! Woof!' That's how I got my dog licence. The girl, like nearly every member of the Government, did not know a word of Irish, nor is there any evidence that any member of this far-from-silent feline service knows, a thing about the legal aspects of her duties.

*　　*　　*

The Minister for the time being? Usually a lovely cut of a man, but what does he DO? It might be imagined that he keeps messing about with the radio station but I do not think that is true. In any case, it has been announced that the station is soon to be detached from the postmen. What then COULD he be doing?

And by the way – why doesn't Radio Eireann give us a production of Harold White's opera *Shaun the Post*?

P.A.

The pathological significance of the nickname has not got its due – certainly not from the University of Harvard, famed inventors of James A. Joyce.

The point about a nickname is, so to speak, its nick. One can throw out of the window the whole wonderland of tedious, contrived literary craft purporting to portray people – fictional people, dead people, even live people – and confess that some dreadful, illiterate guttersnipe has said it all in just one word. Simple (and therefore terrible) things do not lend themselves to exegesis. Love, hate, fear, death – these are all monosyllables. Even lust does not falter in its monosyllabic horror.

Another monosyllable occurs to me: WAR!

I hope I will not be thought uncivil to invite readers not to write inviting my attention to tea, milk, dog, cat, man, bread, and various other commodities which beset the path of every philosopher.

Of such considerations we have heard. We make no comment.

* * *

The preceding somewhat ponderous remarks arise from a conversation I had no later than yesterday. Friday. (You doubt me? Check the calendar?) I knew instantly that my an-, pro-, or even contagonist was a person who engaged, profligately, recklessly, in deep thought. A frown acquired possibly at the age of five, majestically furrowed his brow. He was a person who thought about everything, always very deeply.

I took the only counter-action possible in this grim circumstance. I decided to be deeper.

Let it be confessed that a small technical hitch occurred just then. I did not know how to organise an intellectual frown on my brow. If there had been an attendant there to say: 'Here's the twenty cigarettes you asked for, sir – that'll be two and fourpence', the frown would dawn automatically.

That attendant did not appear. No fault of his, either: it happened I was smoking cigars.

* * *

I done my level best, however I done it: I conveyed an impression of enormous worry, said we would have to get together, sink old differences (ignoring the fact that I knew they were unsinkable) and said something would have to be done about the corners.

My interlocutor was as surprised as you, reader, in this unexpected change of subject.

'Now look,' I said. 'Let's get down to this. Face facts. Why don't you do something about facts instead of privately squawking about them to me. I'm not even a Civic Guard.'

'Not at all. I admire you for your interest in public affairs. What is your remedy for this appalling situation in which we find ourselves?'

'I've told you. Corners.'

'I've been told in the Technical School about corners. They can be inverse and obverse. You can have all sorts of corners. I know that. So what?'

I dare not continue this account in *oratio recta*. To the persistent inquiry as to why I thought that corners was my notion to the solution of the country's endemic ills, I kept saying:

'The boys are there, aren't they?'

* * *

My friend, not realising what I was talking about, clearly was in need of enlightenment in the Indicative Mood.

I said: 'Part of the structure of our contemporary republican civilisation is that such agricultural labourers who are not resident in Dublin civil service offices spend their time in bed judging ladies' fashions.' (I like to think of the exigency of the peasant who, on a most expensive long-distance telephone call with a big Dublin paper, says: 'What sort of a barn do you think I have? It used to contain a mowing machine. Where do you think I am supposed to store the 18 Morris Minors, the 197 Volkswagens, the 18 pianos, and the 1,859 sets of plywood bedroom furniture? What do you take me for? An Irishman?'

What I am attempting to bring you back to, reader, is my opening remark of today. Admittedly, it has been a long way round; namely, that a nickname can be mystical and interpretive, it can explain, it can be the answer.

I said: 'Why can't the Minister for Local Government do something about this situation of economic havoc?'

'The who?' asked my adversary.

'The Minister for Local Government. Your man in the Custom House, below on the kays?'

'Is it Pa you are talking about?'

'Yes, I suppose so. Pa.'

'Pa?'

'Pa.'

Blarney and Baloney

A fellow named Earl Wilson writes a column in the *Richmond Independent*. Don't ask me which Richmond, because there are eighteen of them in North America. The title of his column on St Patrick's Day was 'What Baloney and Blarney?' He talks of St Paddy's Week and having discovered 'in the Mick of time' that the Irish had humour. This was a 'shtartlin' discovery'. An Irishman told him he hoped there would be no tragedies in connection with the festival.

'I had a cousin in last year's New York parade,' he said, 'who forgot to make a left turn and wound up in the East River. 'Twas the only water he touched all day.'

Explaining 'Oi'm half Irish meself', an tlarla Wilson then defines blarney by parable. A Paddy gives up his seat in a bus to a lady, who exclaims, 'You're a jewel!'

'No lady,' says the Irishman, bowing. 'I am a jeweller. I set jewels.'

An Irish farmer was told that a newspaper advertisement would cost two dollars for the first insertion and one dollar for the second.

'Faith,' he said, 'I'd rather put it in the second time now and see about the first time afterwards.'

And so on and so forth. Oi don't mind saying.

* * *

Count me not among those who get angry to see the Irishman regarded as a joke. He is, in fact, no less a joke than any other human, even if he is picked on more often, and vocables like 'Oi' attributed to him by persons who cannot themselves speak English at all. If one wishes, however, to make riposte one has only to consult the massive archive known as 'Cruiskeen Lawn'. There is an answer there for everything. Here is something apropos which appeared ten golden years ago, bedad!

* * *

The scene is a tobacconist's shop in Piccadilly. An American enters, a cigarette lighter in his hand, and is greeted with an expectant bow by the Englishman behind the counter.

AMERICAN: Wyve gotta lighter yearat dunt click, nawanta getsum filler fewye gotny.

ENGLISHMAN: Ehbegy' pahdon?

AM.: I thought mebbe yuddava machine in year – some sorta gadget. (*Shows lighter.*)

ENG. (*sees lighter*): Eh – y'lightah! Quait. Desseh it wants petrol.

AM. (*thinking other doesn't understand*): Allawanta getusum filler – sforma lighter, see. Fadsum plain gas attuddo.

ENG. (*uncomprehending*): Dessehts a bit dry. Wants a bit of petrol. We've got it in tins – ehmentseh tisnt trailly petrol – f'yoad like——

AM. (*not understanding a word*): I dunt thinkya get thydy. (*Looks round.*) Fewadsum canza filler – gasisokay inna pinch – ya see——

ENG. (*decides it isn't petrol customer wants*): Of coahse tmight be the flint wants changing – asmeffact tisnt toll likely——

AM. (*helpless*): This swatawant, see——

ENG.: Ehbegy' pahdon?

AM. (*waving his hand in desperate resignation*): Sokay. Letutgo. (*He starts to leave, wearily.*)

ENG. (*feeling so frightfully unnecessarily disobliging*): Eh – railly cahnt quait, ehmentseh, as the French seh, *je ne comprends pas*—— (*The American turns quickly on hearing this and walks rapidly back to the counter.*)

AM.: *Parlez-vous français?*

ENG.: *Un peu, oui – mais——*

AM.: *Ah, quelle chance! Parlons français!*

ENG.: *Alors, qu'est-ce qu'il vous faut?*

AM.: *Ce qu'il me faut c'est un peu d'essence pour mon briquet.*

ENG.: *Ah, ouiouiouioui!* (He produces a can of lighter fluid from beneath.)

AM.: *Ah, bonbonbonbonbonbonbon!*

(They become very French.)

ENG.: *Comme c'est rigolo! Je vous ai demandé tout à l'heure si vous vouliez de l'essence – en anglais.*

AM.: *En anglais? Vraiment?*

(They shake with laughter.) *Ça, c'est drôle, vous savez!*

ENG. (filling the lighter): *Un peu plus?*

AM.: *Assez, assez! C'est très bien.* (He tries the lighter – it works.) *Bon! Bon, ça marche!*

ENG.: *Oui, ça marche très bien.*

AM.: *Et maintenant combien je vous dois, monsieur?*

ENG.: *Rien, absolument rien!*

AM.: *Mais, vous êtes trop gentil!*

ENG.: *Pas de tout, pas de tout, mon vieux!*

AM.: *Alors, je vous dirai bonjour, monsieur.*

ENG.: *Bonjour, monsieur.* (They shake hands, bowing.)

AM.: *J'espère que madame votre mère va bien?*

ENG.: *Très bien, merci. Et votre famille?*

AM.: *Très bien, merci.* (Bowing politely.) *Alors, mes remerciements!* (Tipping his hat and bowing profoundly.) *Bonjour, monsieur!*

ENG. (Bowing bounteously): *Bonjour, monsieur!*

(They shake hands again. The American goes out, humming happily.)

Future Tense!

O vitam miseram! Majusque malum, tamdiu timere, quam est illud ipsum, quod timetur!

– M. Tullii Ciceronis
Epistolarum Liber X: ad T. Pomponium Atticum:
ex Recensione P. Melii Equulei Cum Ejusdem

Animadversionibus, et Notis Integris Petri
Victorii, Paulli Manutii, Leonardi Malhespinae,
& Aliorum: Amstelodami, MCCCMVI

The cloistered dignity of my editorial labours in another age, the sad sweet frailty of earthly beings, the bittersweet charm of the creature world ever-changing before mine eyes, the grandeur of all effluxions whether of time or water, the *tristesse* of maidens and roses in delicate decay, the glory that was Greece, etc., etc. came together upon me in a poignant visitation of the memory when, chancing to pick up one of the public prints, I read a ministerial allocution on what is called the Free Trade Area.

* * *

Free means 'not being under necessity or restraint, physical or moral; except from subjection to the will of others; not under an arbitrary or despotic government'. The dictionary also alleges that free is allied to friend, and in other languages to love. I do not believe that anything is free, and certainly not trade. Is a tradesman a freeman? But this Free State minister certainly spoke freely, if the report be correct:

The best policy for this country – and it has been Fianna Fáil's policy for many years – is to produce as many of the goods as we previously imported or to produce substitutes for ourselves . . .

Do you mind that now? Read it carefully. It may not be wise but by heaven it's courageous.

* * *

It is difficult to deal with the involved – indeed mystical – concept that is implied in the proposition that goods previously imported should now be produced here. It seems elementary that if goods were imported previously, they are either still here or have been consumed; in neither eventuality doth it appear feasible that those same goods should now be produced here.

Conversely, goods produced here could never have been goods previously imported. Very well. But let me quickly pass from that to the staggering alternative that is suggested. If the Irish, it seems cannot produce goods, previously imported (and I say they cannot) the remedy forsooth, is to produce substitutes for themselves!

* * *

Now I admit this *sounds* all right – but will it work? Can it be done economically? Can . . . can the stuff be got? Won't some of the essentials have to be imported? *And* – where is the logic in asking the Irish to produce substitutes for themselves as an alternative to producing substitutes for imported goods to be consumed by their substituted selves?

Has this thing been costed? Heaven knows I am no mathematician but I have made a few rough calculations and I find that one Irishman, height five feet eight inches, average intelligence, slightly lame in left leg, scar on right forearm, dark hair, slightly greying, *cubes out at £856 the lot*, f.o.r. Dublin!

A better job – and remember that the production of human super-types is a commonplace of contemporary politico-demogenic practice – a better job will run you close on a thousand quid a go. Is it worth it? Can the taxpayer shoulder a posterity so expensive? I take leave to doubt it. Truth to tell, I don't believe the thing would work at all, and the whole idea seems basically irreligious.

Mind you, it may be that I have taken the thing up wrong. The phraseology is ambiguous.

The intention may be, not that the Irish should arrange for their own replacement by sub-human monsters content to exist on imported goods, but rather to engage genuine aliens as substitutes for themselves until conditions mend. Each Irish person, I mean, engage a *locum tenens* while absent in America? Five guineas a week, rising to six, indoor, with car or horse allowance, all fees or super-income to be lodged to the credit of the absentee principal at the 'Chase National Bank, Long Island'?

That at least would be a possibility, and a far better idea than peopling our republic with ersatz acting citizens.

In Darkest Ireland

The following is dead serious. I quote from a lady writer in a Dublin Sunday paper:

Now that the last pre-Lenten pancake has been tossed, rolled up and tucked away, and most engagement lists are as blank as a voting paper for the next election, now is the time to review and revise entertainment schedules.

Sooner or later, and preferably before Easter, etiquette arbiters like Emily Post may get the urge to give some ruling on what has become a burning problem in this domestic help-less era:

Should dinner guests be expected to help with the washing up?

No, you are not supposed to laugh. To use the words of another writer in the same paper, you should remain 'portentious and self important'. (You will look thremendious.)

* * *

But let's see. Mac and the wife Bella have asked myself and my benatee round to a bit of dinner. (The route is always circuitous, the repast fragmentary.) We go, of course. We have to. We guess it will be the usual routine – tinned cheese soup, boxty and fried hake, tepid cider, garlic coffee. And we are right.

There is a pause at the end of the banquet. Bella beams, claps her hands and stands up, fussy as a hen in a hot girdle.

'Let's clear the table and get out to the kitchen,' she says to my benatee. 'I have a new soap powder I simply *adore*!'

My benatee looks down momentarily. She is wearing preposterous gloves reaching to the elbows, a present from Marie Thérèse: no affectation of fashion, though – it is to hide arms irretrievably scalded by thirty years at her own sink. But she stands up. Some minutes afterwards the kitchen door is slammed and we hear sundry commotions within, slightly muted by the hiss of steam as if we were in purlieu of vast laundry.

I have ventured to sit in an armchair with my 'port'. Mac stands up and stretches himself. I notice he is still wearing his bicycle clips.

'Funny thing,' he says. 'See that table. I've just thought of something. The left leg is loose. Reminds me of 1924, when all my teeth got loose. No time like the present. I won't be a moment.'

He goes out and reappears with a small sack of carpenter's equipment. He up-ends the table. Then the hammering starts. In an interval a deafening crash is heard from the kitchen. I notice my 'port' is apparently solidifying.

* * *

I try to look through a stained copy of the *New Yorker* dated 1931. Suddenly Mac collapses into a chair, panting and sweating. I feel I have to say something.

'That job'll be game ball in five minits,' Mac says, 'I'm very handy with the tools.'

I look at a monstrous and apparently deceased dog that is covering the whole front of the fire.

'What do you call him, Mac?' I ask.

'That's Michaelangelo,' Mac says. 'Most intelligent dog in Ireland, I'd say, and a great watch dog. He can nearly talk to you. They're great company, dogs, great company altogether. That reminds me, though . . .' Here Mac frowned. 'He's always eating bad stuff or else some criminal so-and-so is trying to poison him. I wouldn't put it past the Cumann na Gayl crowd to try to strike at me through the dog. Last night he come up to the bedroom and by gob he got sick all over the lovely carpet. I never seen such a mess . . .'

He stopped suddenly, pulled a little shovel out of a coal scuttle, picked up the hearthbrush and handed me the two implements.

'If you wouldn't mind,' he said suavely. 'I'll have the table finished in a jiffy. It's the first room. Second turn right.'

What did I do? I done what I was told.

Golden Boy

There is a traditional affinity between joy and sadness. Tears are caused by laughter as well as sorrow. Animals seem to be immune from either affliction. Any chance of getting ourselves made into animals – discarding this obsession of reviving the Irish language (the current obsession of Mr Seán Lemass) – and becoming dumb?

A few days ago I was attracted to an article in another paper dealing with the pets women keep. Cats predominated. I do not like cats because, unlike dogs, they are secret beings. But the article in question had some photographs, one lady being shown wearing on her shoulder no gaudy ornament, no brass buttons, no epaulet, but what seemed to the uninstructed to be a young rat.

I know better. I immediately recognised the golden hamster. One of the funniest incidents I ever contrived involved one of those little animals, and my reference above to sadness is due to the fact that the man who lent me one for a few hours in a pub is dead.

*   *   *

My friend's business included dealing in ingenious and often alarming toys made in Central Europe. He would sometimes attend a certain pub in the morning time, in search of some wretch who was trying to 'cure' himself after an unwise overnight potation. My friend would fling down a small brown paper parcel, saying 'There's a present for you', and then elaborately occupy himself with something quite else.

The quaking invalid would undue the twine. The parcel contained a cotton affair as big as the largest known snake, and remarkably like one – but containing a vertebra of powerful springs which had been compressed by the binding of the parcel. When the parcel was undone, this terrible thing leaped to life, often giving the terrified opener what seemed to be a ferocious bite.

It is said that many victims tottered off into taxis to see a doctor, in order to get an injection of the antidote to the bite of the deadly cobra before it was too late.

*   *   *

One day my friend put his hand in his overcoat pocket and placed the image of a little brown animal on the counter. Some of his more recent exhibits had not been very good and, with some impatience, I said: 'O.K. Where's the key? Wind it up and let's see what it can do.'

It would be untrue to say that this 'toy' instantly jumped down my throat, but by a great spring it tried to get down inside the collar of my shirt. It was a golden hamster. I instantly saw the possibility of its immobility, its pretence of inanimateness. I had a date with a terrible bore in another part of the premises immediately.

So I borrowed the hamster as my secret weapon.

*   *   *

He was waiting for me all right. My little assistant was snug in my pocket. The Enemy, after buying a drink, roared:

'Are we all gone mad in this country? Did you read the returns in the *Statist* this week?'

'If you are talking about our adverse balance of trade,' I said, 'I would counsel some caution. A lot of statistics are fallacious and misleading. A major industry throughout the world today is lying to the income tax sharks. This necessarily entails the falsification of industrial and other statistics.'

'Is that so? Why doesn't the crowd here do something about the banks?'

'Excuse me a moment.'

* * *

I withdrew briefly to the corridor. Here, making what I supposed were affectionate sounds, I extracted Mr Hamster, who had resumed his pretence of being asleep. Very carefully I placed him on the brim of my hat, at the extreme back. Then I carefully walked back and rejoined the Man Full of Industrial Indignation.

'And another thing,' he shouted. 'What's all this business about bargains in the drapery trade? If a pair of trousers costs me £3 today, how is it I can get the same article at half the price if I wait till tomorrow, because there is a "sale" on? Whaaa? If you ask me the whole lot of us should be above in the 'Gorman. *And not let out again!*'

'Stocktaking,' I said shortly.

'Stock what? What was that you said? I am beginning to think you are up to your neck in this business yourself.'

'No, I do not engage in industry. I am a gentleman. But I am aware that industry is an intricate science.'

'Intricate, did you say? Intricate? What will you have?'

'A small one.'

'*Intricate?* So is smuggling. So is murder. In——? What was that you said?'

It was here the wonderful and much hoped for thing happened. It may have been caused by the loud, choleric voice. The little hamster got up from his snooze at the back of my hat and quietly strolled around to the front. Here he stood on his hind legs and looked my adversary straight in the face.

I cannot describe the result, beyond saying that the

economist goggled, got as white as a sheet, nearly choked himself with his drink, and was forthwith gone.

* * *

I promise some more stories about this hamster. The hamster takes life easy, likes sleep and heat, and does not seem in behaviour to have a bother on him. But like many a comfortable two-legged creature, he is a pessimist. He is never too sure where his next meal is coming from: he makes certain, without going near the Prudential. If offered a meal, he will eat it gratefully – but he will store his next dinner away in pouches he has in each cheek.

No pot-luck merchant he!

Nostri Plena Laboris

Yes, last Sunday's work was a credit to us all. I am not so much taken with the fact that nearly a hundred thousand persons attended at Croke Park to watch the Kings of Kerry do battle with the Bards of Armagh: it was the fashion that for most of these spectators it was not a sporting event at all but an occasion of pilgrimage and suffering, involving all-night travel and starvation.

It is safe to say that a people who thus so prodigally flock to a football park would even more readily form themselves into an army to repel any new invader who may appear – e.g., the Germans acting under the monstrous provocations of Peadar Cowan at Strasbourg.

I take my own small share of credit for this situation.

* * *

I have watched with interest, and, not entirely unmoved, I have been for the past twenty odd years a close spectator and earnest student of the painful but heroic emergence of a people to full registered nationhood. That has been an experience, an inspiration, a direction, something which keeps one young, some indefinable thing that gives life . . . meaning.

In the great tasks of revival and recreation I have given without stint such poor talents as I may have and could claim (were plaudits and crowns of green bay aught to my taste) immense achievements in the internal reorganisation of those three most fertile national seed-buds, Aiséiri, the Gaelic League and the Irish Dancing Commission. Office work (for such it was) is not romantic, nor does it make possible the bold defiant word, the brave gesture, or the hand tucked stoutly in the surcoat, the head thrown back what time imperishable rhetoric emerges from the golden Irish throat.

Quite so. Just office work, files, conferences, interviewing delegates, wangling rail passes for itinerant evangelists. But it was my choice that this task should become my life work.

* * *

To this life work I did not come empty-handed. Profound knowledge of history, immense curiosity about the universal . . . *Zeitgeist*, why it varies inversely through all its phases as the square on the tangential components of the infra-psychic sub-vedantic world ethos, a morbid awareness of the agonising contrapuntal devices employed in supranuminal orphic emanations, their interpenetration, and the vast mantic adjustments thus necessitated in 'achromatic time'; above all, a sobbing, passionate pity for all sub-humanity in general – and in particular a wry, searing, withered sympathy with those nearly demented bipeds who must ever flounder, with shrill batlike squeaks, in a fungescent Dantesque curfew, where naught can flourish save the terrible swollen aphasia of that most incurable squalor, racial . . . amnesia.

* * *

These are but a few of my qualifications for my grim, self-appointed, unestablished post. Will it be credited that my task is nearly accomplished, my plans fulfilled, the situation such as may be left to lesser men who may ambition to grapple in herculean posture with pointless detail? Yes, such is the truth. The race is run – believe, dear reader, that here I intend no vulgar paronomasia! – my days are drawing to Arklow, pardon me, a close. I have seen all the pictures, visited every branch on my personal bicycle; soon I must pay my bills and say farewell (or better, *slaun lath!*), departing never on this orb ever to return, even for the centenary commemoration of my demise.

* * *

What then have I accomplished? How is it now with the old land, how fare her people? Well, vastly well. So well, in fact, that nameless and unnameable churls can write epistles and address them to our person with the greeting '*A Chara* . . .' a greeting not merely jacobin in its coarseness, but also one for which, in the traditions of our face and tongue – of manners in this context it were obscure to speak – there exists no clear precedent – a greeting which, flouting a divinely instituted hierarchy of human values and setting at naught the dignity of man himself, adumbrates a new 'civilisation' which is to mean merely a slough of revolting loutish amity, a country composed solely of . . . of . . . of . . ., *cáirde*!

Sad, you will say, a deplorable return for all my pains I agree. The funny thing is that I could easily have stamped out the whole rank growth if I had been more mindful of my business. Seeing this *cara* word sprouting all over the place thirty or forty years ago, I took no action. Assumed all the time it was the Greek for 'head' and that the peasants were harmlessly immersing themselves in the 'dear dark head' or some similar canon. Now I know better, but I have no regrets.

J. A. Joyce

I was recently reading once again one of Joyce's short stories from *The Dubliners*, named 'Counterparts'. I had nearly forgotten it, forgotten the fact that it had taken many valuable years to persuade any publisher to think that the great collection of which it was part was worth putting out at all. Joyce was a great master of the banal in literature. By 'banal' I mean the fusion of uproarious comic stuff and deep tragedy. For in troth you never get the one without the other, unless either be fake.

This story 'Counterparts' is concerned with, in its first part, the humiliations and insults offered to a solicitor's clerk by a very repulsive boss, sometimes in the presence of visiting clients. The poor clerk thinks that the best method of therapy for this situation is a visit to the pub. There is one snag – a fairly big one – he has no money. (One might here inter-

polate the witticism 'He has no Mooney'!) But what about
his watch chain . . . and the pawnbroker?

So he pawns the chain and gets six bob.

*   *   *

The centre part of the story is concerned with his feeling of
triumph over adversity, his knowledge that in his pocket he
has six shillings, and his resolve to get completely drunk
when a glass of Guinness plain porter, then stronger than the
present bottle of stout, cost 1d.

He goes to the ordained pub, peopled exclusively by
spendthrifts, touchers, bummers, and every class of ruffian
that even the most fanciful could invent. Characters later to
re-appear in *Ulysses* were there – Paddy Leonard, Nosey
Flynn and a few more. Drink was cheap at the time, with
much favour for hot whiskey, a potion I would not touch
unless already in bed with the cabman's coat over the quilts.

Our poor clerk spends the six bob with the open-handed-
ness of a millionaire. Various tavern tricks are tried out,
including the one which involves Who Is The Strongest Man
Here, or *Who Thinks He Is Strong Enough To Force My Arm
Down On This Counter?* –

The poor clerk in our study, by now brimful of D.W.D.,
Dublin's now extinct malt, takes one look at the pup who is
challenging grun men, leers inwardly and outwardly, and
says he will gladly do so, staking the remnant of the six bob.

Naturally, he loses.

*   *   *

There is a small intervention concerning the clerk's glimpse
of a lady who had an enormous black feather in her hat. He
wanted her on her way out to smile at him, if no more – to
concede that he existed. She did not do so. This really
sickened him.

But these were all smallish tragedies, upon which Joyce
was quietly building the big one. The big one occurs when
our clerk is on his way home on the Sandymount tram,
destitute of his gold watch chain, having been humiliated
about the strength of his arm by a music-hall stripling in a
pub, having only two pence in his pocket, and *realising he is
not drunk*!

*   *   *

Joyce falls down slightly at the end of this story, in his attempt to heighten his condition of tragedy. He makes a mistake, to me, quite unexpected.

In those days, the pubs closed at eleven o'clock. (*Inexpertus liquor!*) When this poor man gets home, he finds no dinner awaiting him, and shouts to the upper rooms for his wife without response – 'a little sharp-faced woman who bullied her husband when he was sober and was bullied by him when he was drunk.'

There is nothing to eat, and the kitchen fire is nearly out. He finds one of his small sons, Tom, and demands to know where his mother is.

'She's out at the chapel.'

Such a situation is, of course, impossible. I will not carry my brief recount of this story to the end, but Joyce was, like myself, a great man. The little boy Tom got a terrific thrashing from the bemused clerk, really because of the abuse the latter had that morning received from his boss.

Be Careful!

Next to alcoholism, infanticide, capital punishment and the end of the world, I doubt if there is any one other subject about which more blather is talked than the question of safety on the roads.

Before I proceed further on this dangerous thoroughfare, I should like to refer to a mention in this paper's *Review and Annual*, issued just after Christmas, concerning automobile finance. After some preliminary chat about the extent to which hire purchase is inflationary, the writer was reassuring about the car business. He said that, after inquiry, he had found that only about twenty per cent of new cars were hire-purchased.

A few people in the trade to whom I mentioned this unexpected statistic looked at me hard as if what I had said was the preliminary to a dirty story, then laughed and hastily resumed communion with their companion (i.e. a bottle of stout). Eventually a dealer took my query at its face value, laughed immediately, and then said: 'Listen. If a man came into our place inquiring about such-and-such a model and, on being told it was there, said he wanted it at once and put down cash for it, the whole crowd in our place would have heart failure.'

The same trader estimated that eighty per cent were by hire purchase, preceded by a protracted haggle on the question of trade-in.

*　　*　　*

The papers recently had a letter signed by Mr Edgar Deale, Hon. Secretary of the 'Safety First' Association of Ireland (of all places!) concerning safety on the roads. Although I concede that the intention is impeccable, laudable, I think it is a stupid letter. It is even alarming, for it said the association had received 'a favourable hint from Government circles' that a driving test was to be introduced here.

I think it is shocking to see this sort of nonsense solemnly disinterred, dusted and re-presented in 1955. Insofar as statistics afford the basis of the analysis of road accidents, it has been accepted throughout the world for the last twenty years that driving skill has nothing to do with the case, except that seventy-one per cent of car catastrophes involve drivers of exceptional practice and ability. The natural 'show-off' is never to be seen in more prominence than when at the wheel of a car. He cannot even change gear without affrighting the ear of the passerby. He continually 'drives on the horn', assuming that at crossings and dangerous bends a blast on his trumpet will abolish all other traffic, immobilise children, petrify dogs – even get awkward, obstructive buildings out of the way.

Many accidents are attributed to the class known as drunken drivers. In the case of hardly any such driver is driving skill called in question. If it were, it would be logical to expect 'Government circles' to authorise the issue of two certificates – one for ordinary drivers and one for drunken drivers. Most drivers who drink are very skilled. They would pass any test. They are doing so every day in Britain, where they have also to pass an oral exam about traffic rules.

*　　*　　*

In Britain there is a nationwide organisation known as the Royal Society for the Prevention of Accidents. I am afraid its title is unwieldy, and much of its work is more statistical than practical. I have attended two of its annual conferences in London (delegates numbering about fifteen hundred) and read the society's publications. I emphasise the word 'accidents' in the title: it is not merely 'motor accidents', for the society acknowledges that accidents (unpredictable, dangerous, often injurious occurrences) are going on everywhere all the time.

If death by accident be accounted the major desolation, where would you think is (a) the most dangerous place to be, and (b) the safest?

According to the last report I read, the most dangerous place to be is at home. This is no restatement of the ancient joke about the dangers of going to bed, because most people die there. The number and variety of domestic accidents is shocking. A great number of people fall downstairs. A great number of children pull pans of boiling water on top of their heads, or fall into the fire. If a man of some means says: 'Very well. If I am in danger of being killed by a motor car, I will not go out at all. And if I am in danger of falling downstairs and breaking my neck, I will never go upstairs. I will have my bedroom and living room on the ground floor.'

I need hardly say that it is nearly a certainty that the ceiling will fall on him and kill him.

The safest place on earth to be, according to the figures? In a main-line express train proceeding at an average speed of not less than 55 m.p.h. And I am not joking.

*   *   *

Mr Edgar Deale says another thing in his letter which I find far from funny – for I must assume some people will think he knows what he is talking about. This: 'In our view the road accident frequency is too high, considering the small amount of traffic on Irish roads . . .' Leaving Dublin and a few other spots out of the picture, the high accident rate is to be attributed in the main to sparsity of motor traffic. There are other complications, such as intermittent horse traffic and cyclists, but it is possible to go by road from Dublin to Cork without seeing more than a dozen motor vehicles in motion.

My own plan for reducing all manner of accidents may

seem simple, naïve – poetic, almost. Teach the Irish people
to have manners.

Bicyclicism

Has it ever occurred to the reader that the bicycle has a
personality and a private life? It is the only vehicle I can
think of to which man has deigned to concede the attribute
of sex. We look with equanimity today on the free association
of male and female bicycles. Often I have tried to analyse the
ineffable otherness of female bicycles. Simple folk will tell
you that there is no difference except for the frame and
possibly – in the days of our grannies – the arc of pretty,
protective lacing between the rear mudguard and hub, to
ensure that skirts should not become enmeshed in the
spokes.

But no, it is not a simple question of anatomy. As my
friend Mr James Augustine O'Dea well knows the simplest
way for a man to get a laugh is to go on the stage dressed as a
woman. A far more extreme and less laughable incongruity
is presented by the spectacle of a man riding a lady's bicycle.
He seems to be all knees, self-conscious and diffident of
manner, and aware that he is engaged in obscure man-
oeuvres, I always look away in demure, nunlike evasion.

*   *   *

I have just read with special attention the report of a Roscommon court case in the *Connacht Tribune* which seems to
add somewhat to our scant knowledge of the cyclic universe
which the philosopher Vico tried to investigate. *Cherchez la
bicyclette fatale!*

A man was charged with taking a bicycle without the
consent of its owner (bicycle male, owner male) and also
with taking a bicycle without the consent of the owner
(bicycle female, owner female). One can here sense the
ingredients of drama. To state concisely what happened, I
cannot do better than quote:

Defendant told the Justice that he came to Roscommon for the
races. He took the wrong bicycle home with him, but did not
know that until next morning. The bicycle he took was a man's

bicycle and the one he found he had next morning was a lady's bicycle.

SUPT.: He took a man's bicycle home and left it outside his house. Next morning the owner came along on a bicycle belonging to his sister—— He took his own bicycle and left his sister's.

DEFENDANT: And when I got up I took it to where I thought I took it from. (*Laughter.*)

I must accept that the Superintendent knew what he was talking about, but I do wish the evidence had stopped at the end of the first paragraph. Mundane explanations notwithstanding. I am convinced that here we have a glimpse of dread gynandromorphism.

* * *

The learned Justice fined the defendant 10s and said it was clear the latter had been ingesting what is known in the Paw-Nay argot as stilumants. The background of the occurrence was a race meeting. The Superintendent elucidated the circumstances further. I quote: 'The defendant's own bicycle was locked in a shed in Roscommon and he could not get it out. When he left the bicycle back, another person took it.'

Another man was charged before the same court. A Guard said this man had taken the female bicycle from where the first man had left it. Questioned, this second defendant 'admitted taking it and went to the country for a spin and came back intoxicated'.

But perhaps I have said enough concerning this strange episode.

Neus Papers

Nearly every day I buy Beaverbrook's *Daily Express* out of curiosity to find which of its repertoire of tantrums is being aired, what basket of dirty linen is being washed, what paroxysm enspasms the editor. What mad pursuit? What struggle to escape? What popes and tumbrels? What wild ecstasy?

The latest Empire betrayal concerns the sale by shameless British ministers of the Trinidad oilwells to America. I am not personally too sure about that. Trinidad was in fact discovered in 1498 by Christopher Columbus, who might fairly be described as the first white-skinned American. It was forcibly taken from the Spanish by the British in 1797. The U.S. may not be entitled to exploit Trinidad's oil resources, but it is more entitled to do so than is Britain.

THAT, HOWEVER, is by the way. My confession that I read the *Express* pretty regularly seems to make my private residence a small flat in Queer Street. How do YOU judge another man? By the cut of his clothes, his accent, his manners, his taste in liquor or music, his political beliefs, the quisiteness or exquisiteness of his wife? No, these things are all irrelevant. The *Express* explains that a man is to be judged by the paper he reads, and has described a most meritorious character which it names the DAILY EXPRESS MAN. Apparently I am one of them myself, and the revelation will come as a great shock to my readers, just as it did to myself. Know what Myles is? I quote:

HE TENDS to earn more than £800 a year and is more than likely to be more than £1,300 a year. Only one man in every four you meet is listed in the middle and upper income brackets – but the odds are nearly 50–50 that such men are Daily Express Men.
HE HAS his own business; he is a lawyer, doctor, accountant, high-salaried clerical worker, qualified teacher, director or manager.
HE HAS a small family with one or two children, is more likely than not to own his own house, is more likely than the average man to be running his own car.

In the same issue there is a description of a man who rode to Ascot in a Rolls and there 'sat sipping champagne in a private box'. It was not his own Rolls, for the outing came about because he had won an *Express* competition, and was there a DAILY EXPRESS MAN, like me. But, bless me, it is revealed that he is 'a £10-a-week carpenter'!

A CERTAIN SPECULATION is inevitable. I hereby invite readers to let me have their guess on the subject. *What manner of creature is the* IRISH TIMES MAN? A vexatious Sisyphean inquiry, that. I will here venture my own timid diagnosis.

HE TENDS to earn less than £500 a year so far as the income tax inspector is concerned, but in his apparently crippled shop keeps two sets of books, one for his own information solely.

HE HAS his own business but does hardly any real work himself; he is a civil servant, an Abbey actor, a T.D., a mayor or lord mayor, a pint drinker, a *thooleramawn*, a Gael, a gombeen man, a *gawshkogue*, a patriot, a fearful bore.

HE PRETENDS to regard with great interest and worry questions such as emigration, afforestation, agriculture, reform of income tax law, the return of the Lane pictures (which he thinks were painted by Hugh Lane), and Partition.

HE HAS a small family of ten children and a crippled aunt, owes rates and is more likely than the average man to run his own scooter.

IT IS VERY confusing, though, to have a partitioned personality – to be simultaneously an IRISH TIMES MAN and a DAILY EXPRESS MAN, to say nothing of being also that fastidious cellarman, a cork examiner.

Dramatis Personae

Somebody – I think it was Mr de Valera – was recently discussing education and the competence of our teachers. He deplored the attitude of parents, who expected too much. 'You cannot expect our schools to turn out young Aristotles at the age of fourteen,' he declared.

Fair enough, but the assertion is not quite true. The thing was done at least once, probably many times.

The lad's name was, of course, Aristotle. The Greek root here is concerned with artistry and the production of excellent children. The name is complimentary, and was probably borne by many other schoolboys of fourteen. The real question is – can each of our teachers not be like Aristotle's teacher, Plato?

* * *

This Greek reference turned my mind to Euripides, and thence to the drama in general. Whence this Irish phrase of ours, 'acting the goat'? That is, roughly, what the word *tragedy* actually means, though it is argued that the goat in question was a sacrificial one offered in expiation to certain

angry gods, Dionysius in particular. The derivation reminds
us that in ancient times, and up to times not so ancient, the
drama was a form of divine worship; both Paul Vincent
Carroll and Seán O'Casey seem to realise this and would
like to restore the *status quo*, for they find it very hard to
keep priests out of their plays.

* * *

Every great dramatist realises that there is nothing involved
in the drama except *character*. Some small concession must
be made to theatre-goers, who are usually weak-minded
folk, so that some plot is necessary, no matter how perfunctory or silly. Scenery, costumes, music, whiskey, bars –
these are quite extraneous. *Hamlet* is one of the few of his
plays for which Shakespeare appears to have devised the
'plot' himself, and who else but he could get away with such
nonsense? If a Hollywood man dared to end a film with the
absurd carnage which concludes *Hamlet*, even in Vista-
Vision, he would be very severely derided and scolded, his
picture would probably be banned and compared to those
corrupt 'comics'.

* * *

The Abbey Theatre is offering a 'prize' of £100 for a new
play, I believe. Apart from the objection that the proper
typing of a full-length play would cost nearly that, it means
more priests, kitchens, farmers' wills, a dispute over land
and a murder, perhaps. The prize should be at least £500,
but subject to the condition that no new character may be
used. The best characters have already been established by
the masters, so why try to better them? New *activities* may,
of course, be ascribed to them, but they must be activities-
in-character: thus, a play which includes Iago and which
causes him, before the end, to become a Carthusian monk
would be summarily rejected.

I cannot see why a skilful writer could not combine, in one
new play, the best characters in Shakespeare and Euripides.
Could not Macbeth be married to Medea, for instance?
Could one not, by an inspired misprint, make Hecuba queen
of Tory, not of Troy, and substitute Finn MacCool for,
perhaps, Agamemnon?

If such metamorphic daring seems too extreme, there is

nothing to stop the dramatist from taking characters from various Shakespeare plays and letting them have their fun and crises strictly *inter se*.

Nor need there be any real break with the Abbey tradition. The competition rules could be framed so that the play would have to deal with pre-dictated characters, and they can be as Irish as you like. Here is a suggested cast I have worked out:

> Bould Phelim Brady (a bard of Armagh)
> The Darlint Gil (a Clare lady)
> Ned of the Hill (a mountainy man)
> O'Thello (one of the Moores of Ennis)
> Antonio (a merchant of Ennis)
> Kelly (a boy from Killane)
> Cassius (a Thin Man)
> Peter (a packer)
> Kitty (a Coleraine lady)
> Mary Rowe (one of the Rowes of Tralee).

No one will say that scope is lacking there. O'Thello and Antonio could compete for the local Darlint Girl, with Bould Phelim Brady nicely adjacent to play at the wedding, Peter to deal with the going-away baggage, and a wedding party at which Kelly falls madly in love with Mary Rowe. I imagine Cyril Cusack would make a good fist of that Kelly part, and Mary Rowe – well, of course there's no question *at all* about that, Siobhán McKenna.

León Árd Ó!

What manner of man is Moylan? I don't want anybody to tell me – I *know*. Decentest man that ever wore a hat *but is he qualified to be Minister for Education*? Was he ever at school – TEACHING, I mean, of course? I had better get to my point before I get round to asking about the qualifications of Mr Paddy Smith, a small farmer from wee Cavan, to be in charge of the gigantic metropolitan ganglion known as Dublin. I only ask the reader to get a hold of the satchel of any schoolboy, young or old, and examine the contents; he will be unpleasantly surprised to find that the school world has changed very little since he himself was a boy and cherishing as his heroes Macredy and Harvey Duclos, the cyclists.

I won't go into details, such as listing the English poems still appearing in 'approved' anthologies for intermediate students – 'Lochinvar', 'Rosabelle', 'A Psalm of Life', 'Destruction of Sennacherib' – all calculated to debauch burgeoning taste. The volumes containing Gaelic contain shocking trash. Generally speaking, school-going folk are still regarded as morons. It is a good job our educationalists cannot disturb the historic equation $2 + 2 = 4$, though with the preposterous system of Gaelic numerology still burnt with acid into youngsters' minds (16 men = *seisear fhear déag*) it is possible to go very near sabotaging the third R.

Why are there no interesting, elevating and truly educative books 'on the course'? What, for example, would be more valuable for intermediate and senior students than an illustrated study of Leonardo da Vinci, in whose life painting, sculpture, engineering, architecture, mathematics, music and philosophy were so wonderfully met?

Such a study would be an inspiration as well as an education: therefore it is out of the question.

*   *   *

This space in this instance denotes the passage of two hours for I have been glancing through Forster's edition of some material from Da Vinci's famous note-books. Certainly Da Vinci was what we usually call an extraordinary genius. In many instances he shows for the first time the way to do certain useful but very difficult things but, as a matter of pride and virtuosity, sees no harm in explaining how extremely unuseful things may also be done. Example:

If you wish to make a fire which shall set a large room in a blaze without doing any harm, you will proceed thus: first perfume the air with dense smoke of incense or other strong smelling thing, then blow or cause to boil and reduce to steam ten pounds of brandy. But see that the room is closed altogether, and throw powder of varnish among the fumes and this powder will be found floating upon the fumes; then seize a torch and enter suddenly into the room and instantly everything will become a sheet of flame.

You see? Here is a man so sophisticated that he thinks nothing of getting his brandy dry – and by the pound!

He has another rather queer plan which might be defined as how to get fresh air the hard way, with benefit of eerie, pneumatic clothing:

It is necessary to have a coat made of leather with a double hem over the breast of the width of a finger, and double also from the girdle to the knee, and let the leather of which it is made be quite air-tight. And when you are obliged to jump into the sea, blow out the lappets of the coat through the hems of the breast and then jump into the sea. And let yourself be carried by the waves, if there is no shore near at hand and you do not know the sea. And always keep your mouth at the end of the tube through which the air passes into the garment and draw . . . from the air within the coat.

I wonder what he means by 'obliged to jump into the sea' and 'you do not know the sea'? He seems here to be anticipating the present-day 'frogman' technique but somehow I wouldn't fancy my situation if that leather monkey-jacket sprang a leak. Even without a leak, it seems a risky class of a bathing suit. But it must have worked in Da Vinci's day, otherwise he would not have suggested it on paper. He tested his goods.

He devised several kinds of clocks. Here is how he describes one of his ingenious water clocks – and can't you see a fascinated schoolboy hurrying home to make a similar?

A clock to be used by those who grudge the wasting of time. And this is how it works – when as much water has been poured from the funnel into the receiver as there is in the opposite balance this balance rises and pours its water into the first receiver; and this being doubled in weight jerks violently upwards the feet of the sleeper, who is thus awakened and goes to his work.

It is odd to think that Leonardo is . . . dead. There is no trace in the note-books of any machine to deal with *that*. Could it be that this great enemy of boredom laughed himself to death?

I wonder would Moylan like to borrow my copy of the

note-books? I'll throw in a few of my own as an extra inducement, if need be. All I ask is that growing schoolboys should be introduced to the greatest intellects as early in life as may be.

A Holy Shew

They say that god does not eat god. I wouldn't like to bet on that. I have been noticing with deep disquiet for some time that when our own music correspondent wants to write the word show, he writes shew. What weird foible, what parasceuastic symptom of mental twilight have we here?

Our critic C.A. is by no means alone in his infirmity. My own first contact with shewmanship was many, ah many golden years ago when the grannie (fine figure of a woman, always wore dyed bits of lace curtain tied under the chin to keep her hat on) sent me as a boy to the Brothers – or *Aos Leathair* as I used to secretly call them, split infinitive an' all. It was there I encountered Messrs Hall and Knight, who wanted me to 'shew that a circle having a radius of 4 has more than twice the area of a circle having a radius of 2' or something equally asinine. From that day I associated 'shew' with pomposity, preciosity, pretence of learning, affectation of austerity.

* * *

Please permit a small digression. The next time I encountered 'shew' it was in a different book by Hall and Stevens. What on earth had happened to Knight? I remember deciding that, whereas Hall was a dull, plodding but accurate pedagogue, Knight was a brilliant mathematician – *but* given to taking such sups as made him go homewards in his beloved circles. The momentous breach with Hall occurred when Knight's bleary voice was heard coming up the road where the two savants had their digs. He was singing:

> Shew me the way to go heme
> I'm tired and I wanna go to bed,
> I had a little drink about an hour ago
> And it's gone right to my head;

> Wherever I may roam
> On land or sea or foam
> You will always hear me singing that song
> SHEW ME THE WAY TO GO HEME.

Mind you, we have all our little temptations to cultivate an eclectic attitude to language. Thus do we signify our nobility, spurning the common coin. I well remember travelling all Ireland as manager of a fit-up stage outfit – we had Jimmy O'Dea, Wilkie Collins, Hamar Greenwood, Seamus, the Bird, Harvey Duclos, Barton McGuckin and Cathal McGarvey. On the last night in Bagenalstown Wilkie Collins, whom we had appearing in *A Royal Divorce*, got very drunk and pale with anger, complained to me that his part had been ruined because a window-cill, which was supposed to be glistening, was in fact plastered with muck which had seriously soiled his fancy clothes and drawn laughs. The scenery had already gone to our next pitch, Carlow.

I sent this telegram to our baggage man, conveying that the nuisance of the company was sick and very angry, and that the window-ledge should be polished till it shone:

99 557 443. 201 499. 1,011 994, 201 488 – Roman.

You don't get it, I suppose? Shows how all this TV, spring 'collections', espresso coffee and rock 'n roll have atrophied the cerebral antennae of the civil decent people who read this newspaper. The signature 'Roman' is, of course the clue. The message was:

ILL DIVIL LIVID. CILL DIM. MIX VIM,
CILL VIVID.

J. J. & Us

Recently a chap said to me: *How's it going?* I told him it was going so-so. Slow of course. These things take time. None of your up at seven in the morning and nine times round the track before breakfast with Johnny Morton hidden in the hedge with a stop-watch in his claw. Uphill work when all decent Christians are in bed. The midnight oil. Drudgery of a special kind.

Told you. Bit off more than you could chaw. You and all that B. Comm. crowd is too smart.

No, no, no, I told him. The job COULD be done. There were, of course, difficulties – minute things of rhythm, luminance, impact. The acute difficulty in translation lay in the lucid conveyance of obscurity. Even the hidden thing was susceptible of diacrisis. Not in the same darkness were all dark things enwrapped.

Far as I'm concerned there's no future in that class of thing at all. You'd be a damn sight better off playing the bagpipes in Bagenalstown.

A bit testily (I admit) I asked him to judge for himself. I read out this sentence:

Ineluctable modality of the visible: at least that if no more, thought through my eyes. Signatures of all things I am here to read, seaspawn and seawrack, the nearing tide, that rusty boot ...

Then I read from my large manuscript:

Mionshamhlíocht dosheachanta an tsofheicse; fiú an mhéid sin féin, intiníocht tré fháisnéis súl. Lorg an uile a bhfuil agam annso le sonnrú, scéag mara, leathach, an tuile i gcuaird, an bhróg úd mheirgeach ...

Know what. It's getting damn near half ten. See you in the morning.

*   *   *

I suppose uncertainty is the handmaid of all grandiose literary projects. Many motives lay behind that 1951 decision of mine to translate Joyce's *Ulysses* into Irish. If they won't read it in English, I said to myself, bedamn but we'll put them in the situation that they can boast they won't read it in Irish aither.

It's *work* though. And black thoughts encloister me, like brooding buzzards. Is it worth being accurate if nobody will ever read the translation? What's the Irish for Robert Emmet? And who will put Irish on this fearsome thing written by Joyce himself: *Suil, suil, suil arun, suil go siocair agus, suil go cuin?*

See the snares in this business, doom impending, heart-break?

* * *

I'm nobody's fool, of course. I know that some other body may beat me to it. I have seen with anxiety that Joyce's *Dubliners* has been issued by the Penguin people, price half a crown. How do I know that they are not secretly incubating a cheap *Ulysses*, a *Finnegans Wake*?

I have often been thankful for the title of that last mentioned book for, hard up for a jeer, I have quoted here by name the learned men who have criticised and reviewed it and yet called it *Finnegan's Wake*. That is the title as it is cited on the Penguin *Dubliners* inside and outside. Put it down to negligence or ignorance. But what word have we for this thing, on p. 128?:

> Mr Lyons sat on the edge of the table, pushed his hat towards the nape of his neck and began to swing his legs.
> 'Which is my bottle?' he asked.
> 'This, lad,' said Mr Henchy.

That comma after 'this' – have we a word for it? Yes: BLASPHEMY.

Failure

Recently I made a heroic resolution, but failed shamefully to implement it. *I resolved to write or say absolutely nothing about the cold!* I felt enough people were discussing the matter.

Nor was my resolution hasty or rash. I knew that I would have to 'sublimate' my physical awareness of all the en-girdling snow and ice, and even take note of the possibility of having my face put in by a frozen snowball. I decided to visit a suburban picture house, knowing it had a good heating system. I did not bother to find out what picture they were showing.

After they had thrown on the screen the customary invitation to the patrons to fill themselves with ice cream,

I lit a cigarette, heated my face for a minute or so with my exuberant petrol lighter, and settled down for the entertainment.

* * *

First came the newsreel.

It gave us elaborate and indeed gruesome details of the avalanches in Austria, with shots of frozen corpses being disinterred. It is a fact that the glare of the snow and the perished-looking rescue parties caused a distinct drop in my faltering temperature. I put on my gloves and turned up the coat collar. I was relieved to see that news reel off to something else – a sunken Comet, I think. After a while the main picture came on. Guess what? *The Ascent of Everest.* I shuffled my feet to see whether I was wearing crampons.

I must confess that this is a good picture but also declare that parts of it bored me. The men it showed were heroes, their enterprise most laudable, their physical endurance much to be commended, but they were persistently engaged in climbing a mountain that was some seven miles high, and I thought there was a numbing sameness about the task – one damn peak after another.

I have not read Major Hunt's book on the expedition, but I was much puzzled by the ending of the picture. I confess that I was harbouring a malicious hope that there would be a tremendous Technicolored climax, showing Hillary and Tenzing planting the Union Jack on top of the world, notwithstanding the fact that only the two were credited with making the complete assault. They are shown disappearing from view into swirls of mist and snow, and re-emerging later making jubilant gestures to their anxious friends.

I accept that they did the job, of course, but there should have been more exposition of the meteorological record of the achievement, if only for the instruction (no names!) of an odd person who might take it into his head to make the climb in the future.

* * *

I emerged, frozen, wondering why snow is so unsatisfactory when photographed in colour, and whether a bottle of stout would do me any harm. Intrepid, just like those mountaineers, I entered a strange tavern, ordered my drink and began to think furiously. It was then I made my resolution: NOT A WORD ABOUT COLD!

But what was I going to write about today? Would it be considered affectation to ignore this arctic blight that was residing in my bones? No, I decided – provided one could think of some really important alternative theme. Then I had it; the day saved: *I would start a rumour that this fancy £650,000 Dublin road would bypass Bray as well!* That would be something to shout about from Luxembourg.

*   *   *

But I reckoned without fate. Two men were sitting near me. They conversed as follows for twenty minutes:

I never seen such weather in me life.

You can say that again. I was fool enough to get out on the bike this morning. Well look at.

Did you come down?

I got a toss that nearly killed me. I was picked up by a Free State Army private.

It's freezing NOW, of course – you know that?

Of course it's freezing now.

Do you know what I'm going to tell you . . . ?

One of the men eventually said farewell. *I was alone with the other*. I sat there, petrified with fright and cold, my mind in the condition I would attribute to a man kneeling at the guillotine. The blow duly fell.

I suppose, he said to me, that day's cold enough for you, ah?

Yes.

Wait till I tell you what happened me on me way home last night. This crowd of chislers were on the path making a slide. Do you know? Well, do you see that thumb? Do you see the way it's swelled up?

Yes.

That class of carry-on in the streets should be put down. Now wait till I tell you this . . .

(*Collapse of my Excellency.*)

Ravelled Sleeves

How do you read, reader, your newspapers, your daily stint of Homer, your compendium of Cicero's letters to Atticus? Where, I mean – when, and in what physical attitude? On the answers to these questions depends the impact of what you read on your consciousness. Personally I read in bed, both in the early morning and at night – and what a bed, a present from George Moore and which will be on display at the Spring Show. The springs are superb; one might call them the heart of the matter, just as I find the latter's mate (the mattress) very good for the liver.

What is sleep? Disgraceful to relate, nobody knows. Nobody can say what is the relation between medical anaesthesia, a fainting fit, and sleep. A few elementary *results* have been noted – depression of the central nervous system, decline in rates of heart action, respiration, and pronounced anaemia in the brain region, and general vascular dilation. It is clear to my hippocratic eminence that there are very many kinds of sleep; a horse often sleeps standing up, for instance; a hen sleeps perilously roosting on a lofty perch, and a dog, stretched out in profound sleep, maintains some emergency radar system which enables him to bound up at the tiniest irregular sound. While man usually sleeps horizontally on what is called a bed, he also finds it easy to sleep in a chair; indeed, a chair confronting a desk covered with work papers often induces profound, refreshing slumber. There is an old story about the office worker who apologised to his boss for turning in late, explaining he had overslept. 'Good heavens,' the boss cried, 'you don't mean to say you sleep at home too!'

I wonder is there any connection between Hippocrates and *hypnos*, the Greek for sleep?

* * *

It is generally held that sleep is a 'natural' occurrence and that people who are asleep are behaving normally, if not rationally. Some doctors hold that while sleep is not bad for you, it is by no means essential so long as you go to bed and rest. I do not agree with this. Wakefulness inhibits complete relaxation of the brain and muscle, and the salubrious diminution of metabolism; I say nothing of the fact that many people who should be asleep spend the night watches drinking cider and smoking twenty cigarettes, often achieving disastrous demolition of the sleep of friends by use of bed-side telephone. This fellow is a very distinctive personality, and I hold that many strange things can be explained by reference to whether the subject sleeps badly or not at all.

Medical men are agreed that even in normal quotidian wakefulness, many sections of the brain are asleep. A man cleaning the sparking plugs of his car is not considering Mozart's music. This function of cerebral concentration is very much stepped up at night, and the sleepless thinker occupies his anaemic head with some obsession and often reaches conclusions which he would never reach by day. Wherefore, any person who is found to be awake in the small hours of the morning should be suspected: very likely he is up to a little bit of no good.

* * *

It would be tedious to quote some of the innumerable references to sleep in the world of literature, or show what an obsession the subject of sleep itself has been, and its meto-nymic function as a paraphrase of death. *Nam videbar somniare, memet esse mortuum*, Terence says. (Actually, are *mors* and Morpheus connected?) Cicero, Horace, Ovid and indeed the whole bunch of those fellows were never done blathering about the occult meaning of the *somnium*, or dream. Plato and his butty, Aristotle, were disorderly in the same regard. Nearer home, Shakespeare dragged the sleep theme into most of his plays, and otherwise incurred notice by dragging his second-best bed into his will, which he probably made in bed.

There is a cognate question we must consider some day: are people who cannot sleep incapable of dreaming? And if so, does this imply a critical deficiency in their powers of reasoning and imagination when awake by day?

* * *

Two men who were desperately bad sleepers were Einstein and Hitler. I think Einstein was mischievous and futile. To him is not to be attributed the quantum theory, the concept of the space–time amalgam, nor nuclear fission. Allow him by all means the particularised and general Theory of Relativity, and some other minor researches. And for goodness sake do not remind me that he received a Nobel award, for all such judgments and awards signify nothing more important than Swedish presumption. W. B. Yeats was awarded a prize for literature, and last year his work was equated with that of the most fearsome of all the American literary slobberers, Hemingway.

Einstein's Theory is just that – a theory, an explanation of the universe in novel terms; it has no practical application, though it could induce spiritual necrosis in some students of it. There has been some antiphonical wit on this subject as follows:

> Nature, and Nature's laws, lay hid in night:
> God said, *Let Newton be!* and all was light.
> > – *Alexander Pope.*

> It did not last: the Devil, howling *Ho!*
> *Let Einstein be!* restored the *status quo.*
> > – *J. C. Squire.*

Professor Synge, of the Dublin Institute of Advanced Studies, seems, in a letter to the Editor, to wish to take me to Tasque, County Antrim, in respect of some sober remarks I made about Einstein last week. The Professor's letter really involves a severer criticism than any of mine. I promised to go into this matter deeply but am held up temporarily for want of the Minowski typographical symbols, and by my plan to elucidate an affinity I seem to detect between certain aspects of the Einstein Theory and the tuning of the violin in fifths.

In the meantime, I recommend to the Censorship Board that the circulation of all Einstein's published works should be banned in this country. They are no proper reading matter for our young people.

A Shandy Shindy!

I think I have made recently an enormous discovery of public importance, but lack the assurance to be glib about it.

Why, I ask myself, should destiny leave vast discovery to me?

I have a great selection of answers to that sort of question. Did you ever ponder, reader, how more favourably disposed is the answerer to the questioner? Or is it conceivable that you have read nothing about Joan of Arc and the Spanish Inquisition? The questioner always loses. *Quid est veritas?*

*　　*　　*

I don't want to be coy on this subject. Maybe one reason is that the subject is, as I have said, of public importance. I should like to treat of it carefully, slowly, even laboriously.

Picture the scene. Let us say the hour is midnight. I am immersed in my vast bed in Santry. I sleep. Beside me ticks an alarm clock made at least two centuries ago by Cellini.

This ancient tick I do not hear for the good reason that I am asleep. But I had been at OKLAHOMA the night before on a free pass (I wish to goodness the Education Department would get around to issuing them!) and was awakened at 6 a.m. next morning, which looked to me (in my then state) as wondrous and golden!

OH, WHAT A WONDERFUL MORNIN', I asked myself, springing not only out of the bed but nearly out through adjacent window. It took me what seemed an age to get my man in the distant livery stables on the intercom. 'Get the car round to the front door in five minutes,' I said. 'I want to go for a walk.'

Therein there was really no intent at humour. In that queer complex of castles and parks where I live (Santry) you simply *have* to get the Bentley out to get driven to a point where it is reasonably safe to get out and walk.

I know I have not yet revealed what I am supposed to be talking about. I find that crisis a bit too much. 'Why don't you face up to it and be a man?' Is it reasonable to expect that us Irishmen should for fifty years look like Clark Gable while we are endlessly being congratulated on being married to our own mothers?

Don't think I am unduly cranky today. I confess I am cranky enough but not because today is today.

On that early morning I have mentioned, I believe that I discovered the absolute nadir of Irish vulgarity and pseudo-gentility.

I suppose there will descend on my head nothing but abuse if I assert that there is direct connection and relevance as between Immanuel Kant (German philosopher, b. 1724) and a large shandy (hot weather drink, comp. equal quantities ale and lemonade)?

I seen it with my own eyes. I use those of none other.

* * *

Another day I want to write about this fellow Kant. He was 'an extraordinary genius', which is the conventional Irish term for 'madman'. Aspiring to learn German in the days of my youth, I thought a good idea was to read (however painfully) a book in German. I read Kant's *Critique of Pure Reason* without knowing (really) any German at p. 1, though I knew plenty of German by the time I reached the last page. Waiting for the bus? Waiting for the German verb is surely the ultimate thrill!

I cannot, as I have said, discuss Kant in general just now, but I do wish to say something about how Kant's thought is related to the large shandy.

Kant attempted to define what has long bemused mankind – the distinction between what IS and what SEEMS TO BE. He did not make much real progress in that line of country, particularly because he put his faith in terminology: he seemed to think that if he gave a thing a name, he knew what it was. (This is wrong: if you keep calling a dog a cat, this will never change the dogness of dog.)

Kant, all the same, tried to distinguish between the ascertainable and the illusory, calling things he said existed as *noumena* and what we all imagine exist (that priceless heritage of indestructible hallucination without which we could not go on!) as *phenomena*.

Now let me back to that large shandy.

* * *

I got this fellow who drives the Bentley to transport me away out in the Dalkey direction. I have not been out in that direction for ten years and it was a great revelation to me, all the houses they have built out there. In fact, I was going to buy a few only it was half six in the morning and there was not a soul on view on the roads. Why do so many Irish persons think that THE DAWN is the name of a film made years ago in Killarney by Tom Cooper, rather than a most elaborate, intricate and impressive procedure, staged every morning like the *Irish Times*?

* * *

This shandy is not yet in my hand. The point that myself and Kant seek to make is that the shandy, by reason of its golden transparency, its sheer immensity, its foam, LOOKS cool and therefore – here is the important thing – IS IN FACT COOLING. That concept brings you right back to a system of philosophy founded on the simple idea *I doubt whether I am here at all, so I must be here because I can thus doubt*. (The wise man concerned is no longer here.)

But it is of the essence of the shandy that it is immense, just as a drink of whiskey must be small, sinister, served in vile containers.

* * *

I got lost in the Dalkey–Killiney district on that memorable morning and ultimately found my bearings in the great metropolitine morass commonly called Dun Laoghaire. You can picture me there if you like: the Bentley above in Dalkey and me waiting for a bus.

Then it happened. There was a great clatter across the road opposite me, and a pub began to 'open'. I remembered times past, and marvelled. Nowadays there are no shutters. How do they now bring one's grandfather home on Saturday nights?

Another fellow beat me to it. We both entered a fairly large, fairly filthy, front snug. Without knowing it, we were in the lounge. After my predecessor had ordered a pint of stout and produced the *Daily Herald*, I knew we were not birds of a feather, so I ordered a large shandy, and sat morosely at a distance.

Both orders were wordlessly accepted. It happened that I was served first. I was astounded to see two half-pint glasses being put before me by the unshaven servitor. My unknown companion got the same treatment. *We don't serve pint measures in the lunge*, was the explanation I got.

'You might at least wipe your nose in the lunge,' was all the reply I could just then think up.

Black Friday

A splutter of leaden rain knocked at my window. Twitching the curtain with gaunt pyjama'd arm, I espied a scamper of deadly cloud assembled on one of the nearer horizons. An ill day, I thought to myself. Then there was a knock. My man Shaamus entered with my breakfast. I frowned at the tray. We were, I told Shaamus for the thousandth time, now living in a Republic, and Crown Corks savoured of *lèse majesté*.

'This is a bad, sad day for Ireland, sor, yer honour,' Shaamus said.

'The weather,' I riposted, 'speaks for itself. But why sad?'

'Today, sor,' Shaamus said, 'they are putting the penny on the pint of stout.'

'Very good, Shaamus,' I said. 'I will give you a name for this dark day. Call it D-Day: *dee*-Day. See?'

*   *   *

After Shaamus had closed the door in tactful quietude, I near leapt out of the bed on hearing a Still Small Voice inside my head saying: '*Tis a worse day than you think, sor. Today they're selling your office, the Scotch House.*

Heavenly fathers! Shades of the Old Crowd! There we were in a lump, all in strong body-coats, myself in the lead – Henry James, Bernard ('Barney') Kiernan, Hamar Greenwood, Melfort Dalton, the Bird Flanagan, Jimmy Joyce, Harvey Duclos and MacCredy the cyclist, all heading into the Scotch House for hot tailers of malt, with a clove apiece thrun in to take the smell off our breaths. I remember cuffing a young fellow selling flags in connection with some 'rag', and being reminded by Joyce (who at that time called himself 'O'Halloran') that the da, Gogarty, was an important man.

Them certainly were the days! I remember telling another stripling named Robinson to be off about his business. Little did I guess that the youngster was to become Dr Lennox

Robinson, revered founder of the Abbey Theatre, and a nephew-in-law of my own.

* * *

On realising the day that was in it, I rushed to the telephone to ask my solicitor whether certain important stipulations of mine had been embodied in the Conditions of Sale of the Scotch House. No, nothing had been done. Neither the auctioneer nor the solicitors for the vendor would hear of my requirements. Times had changed, my own solicitor confided to me. Changed they certainly had!

I had asked for merely the following fundamental safeguards – and do not, I pray the reader, too rashly discern in the draughting the cunning hand of my friend Mr E. de Valera!

The Emptors guarantee that insofar as the conduct of the Scotch House hereinafter is concerned, Myles na Gopaleen shall, as a human person antecedent to all positive law, be permitted to pass and re-pass and where necessary pass out on the premises.

Expenses incurred in connection with the supply of glasses of malt to Myles na Gopaleen shall be and hereby are met by the said Emptors, as shall similar expenses incurred at the instance of persons properly designated 'O.S.'.

There shall be constructed and night and day maintained and manned a side-door bearing the letters 'O.S.' through which shall be admitted all persons being, or colourably protesting to being, Old Segotias of the said Myles na Gopaleen . . .

Times indeed have changed. Yesterday morning in the chill of my Santry bedroom, I looked up a book written by my friend of the old days, O'Halloran: or to give him his present title, 'James Joyce'.

* * *

Here is what he wrote, over fifty years ago:

When that round was over there was a pause. O'Halloran had money but neither of the other two seemed to have any: so the party left the shop somewhat regretfully. At the corner of Duke Street, Higgins and Nosey Flynn bevelled off to the left while the other three turned back towards the city. Rain was drizzling down on the cold streets and when they reached the Ballast Office, Farrington [me – M. na G.] suggested the Scotch House. The bar was full of men and loud with the noise of tongues and glasses.

The three men pushed past the whining match-sellers at the door and formed a little party at the corner of the counter. They began to exchange stories . . .

Well, I moseyed along to that auction of the Scotch House in the Gresham Hotel yesterday afternoon. Who will deny the right of the chief mourner to attend the funeral?

Bidding in the Gresham was slow. The ascent of Parnassus or Everest was leisurely compared with what those present had to face when the financial altitude of £30,000 had been reached. Extracting extra bids of £100 was as painful as having bad teeth dug out. But the ultimate winner was Mr Hugo Dolan, for £33,700, who assured that my own rights and those of all 'O.S.' would be eternally safeguarded.

Let us, then, leave it at that. Good luck to the new owner!

Boaoe!

Readers may recall that, when writing about NAMES some weeks ago, I revealed that there was a very queer, not to say vowellent, one to be found at the back of the Latin dictionary, namely(!)

AEAEA

It sounds like a suitable name for a girl, but it must not be assumed that my heading today is the name of the brother. Let me explain.

I was reading an article in a London Sunday newspaper about snobbery, affectations, and all that line of old hat. (The author was a lady, naturally!) The following few lines occur:

I suppose most of us have been stung by the 'little' hotel on the Continent, so fervently recommended, so disastrously un-plumbed. By the 'little' dressmaker. By the back-street wholesale place where 'you can use my name'.

Now I write the names and addresses down obediently on the back of an old envelope and throw it away later.

Can you *now* see what my title means? You are most un-intelligent if you don't.

* * *

There is a mystery involved. I cannot solve it, but it is simple enough to state. *Why are all important or momentous things involving scrivenery always done on the* BACK OF AN OLD ENVELOPE?

You have tangled for a week with an insoluble mathematical conundrum, almost hidden behind mountains of treatises and reference books. It is hopeless. *Can* it be done at all? Very likely not.

Then one night in a pub you meet that mutual friend of ours who notoriously has a head on him. Just to annoy, and possibly humiliate him, you state the problem.

He frowns, thinks for a moment, then produces a pencil and scribbles the correct answer on the back of an old envelope.

Why not? He's only human, isn't he?

* * *

The famous mathematician, Rowan Hamilton, was most eccentric. When he discovered quaternions when taking a walk along the Grand Canal, he broke into a run and scratched the precious formula on the side of a canal bridge. How Celtic, how unBritish!

And how unlike Sir Frank Whittle. Sir Frank was the man who invented the jet engine. On what did he jot down the crude drawings, the rough calculations? On the back of an old envelope. With what? A stub of a pencil, ass!

* * *

Relatively, the atom bomb, the hydrogen bomb, the cobalt bomb – these are things which have changed the whole world utterly within the last ten years. How many, many backs of old envelopes were jotted over in devising those miracles?

People there are who regard them, not as miraculous triumphs of the human intellect, but as horrors of diabolical inspiration. Would it be a remedy to have old envelopes internationally banned?

I doubt it much. It would take superb juridical prowess to attempt even a definition of an old envelope. My own impression is that it must have been through the post, number one. It must be crumpled and soiled through having been carried about in a man's pocket. A *man's*, mind you. A lady carries her letters in her bag, and the envelope, even if carried about there for a year, would be as shapely and clean as the day it was received.

And who ever heard of a wonderful thing being jotted down on the back of a new, unused envelope? That ways lies sacrilege, or something.

* * *

Let us suppose, taking a more constructive view, that people of unique ability should be *encouraged* to help humanity. Here is a man who could achieve prodigies, but nobody likes him, nobody ever writes to him – *he has no old envelopes*: he will probably never have a real one of his own. Must his unique brain be thus forever entombed, his thought turned to stone, his head made a husk?

It looks like it. I had a notion that perhaps it would be a remedy if an enterprising stationer offered old envelopes for sale at a few pence the dozen. I don't think so, though. *The old envelope on the back of which a man of genius scribbles must be his own, addressed to himself by name.* And not BY himself!

That Sunday paper I mentioned, I had long thrown it away when the idea for this excellent article came into my head. The idea was not lost, of course – it came to me on top of a bus, so I scribbled it down on the back of an old envelope.

Well, Boaoe Boaoe!

Electrolocution

I remarked recently that a friend and I, viewing the O'Dea–O'Donovan show at the Dublin Gaiety Theatre, discerned something about the show that was not 'narchrl'. We traced this temporarily unsettling nuance to the fact that no microphones were in use on the stage. We were back, you might say, in the Roman amphitheatre. People speaking used their voices. It was a bold innovation. I have reflected on it and I may tell you they are pretty deep, these waters. Few people are prepared to take the stage human being of today neat, so to speak. The player must be presented through a mechanistical or electronic filter. A live stage show must imitate the film, not vice versa. The player must be a hundred times as large as life; his voice must boom. Indeed, one of the neater acts in the Gaiety show was that of a player going through the digital and brachial paroxysms of the virtuoso pianist though the instrument was a dummy and the pianistic uproar skilfully dubbed. The real person of today's player tends to become a 'source', a myth. I am told now that in America they are experimenting with a telephone which has attached to it a small television screen. When you dial a number, the screen lights up, showing the distant receiver. You hear it ringing. Your lady friend, dishevelled and full of marijuana, totters into the room trying to pull a dressing gown on, yanks up the receiver, and roars 'Yes!?' You might imagine the telephone has enough terrors as things are.

* * *

I went along to the last Horse Show and paused at the stand of a radio firm. They had a television receiver at work. Some play or other, I thought: a rather seedy-looking character was shown in a slouched attitude, apparently waiting for a bus or for some confederate in a vice racket. I waited, and lit a cigarette. So did the fellow on the screen. I threw away the match. So did he. Then I realised that I was looking at myself. High up on the stand a television camera was trained on me. This gimmick became so popular with old and young alike that it had to be switched off from time to time to prevent congestion.

Here is the vital thing: although the TV image was excellent, any of the people who gestured, smiled and frowned to see themselves on the screen could have had an even clearer and more faithful image before a mirror at home; evidentally they felt that there was something mystical, sacramental almost, in achieving a reflection that involved the complicated assistance of miles of wiring, transistors, tubes, switches and electricity. Somewhat the same point was made recently in *Punch* (a London magazine edited by some chap whose name I don't recall, friend of Mr Brendan Behan); a very important person was shown sitting in his carriage in a grand ceremonial procession, but he was watching the procession and himself in his carriage on a television set in his carriage.

* * *

I note also that another dubious, two-edged boon is rapidly growing out of the experimental stage in Britain and the

U.S. This is an 'almost human' yoke which translates matter from one language to another. If it 'knows', say, German and English, you type whatever you want translated in either of those languages. After a very brief delay enlivened with slight noises and the flashing of lights, another machine like the conventional teletype goes into action, quickly typing out an accurate translation of what was fed to it in the other tongue. This great invention has a 'memory' and also 'feelings'. In its present stage of development, it is necessary for anybody testing or interviewing it to play fair and observe plain manners. If you callously type something for translation into a language the machine does not know, you may cause it to have a nervous breakdown, perhaps causing it to be taken away and sent to some sort of an electronic nursing home.

Deep waters, as I said. Sometimes at stage shows, when I am limp with boredom, I am astonished at the torrential applause that greets the fall of the curtain. Hmmm. I have always assumed that the row was caused by the percussion of the palms of those present. Now? Well . . . cynicism is an ugly thing. Let us change the conversation and spend an honest hour with that thing, not new but honest – the gramophone. Who would like to hear Madame Kirby Lunn sing *Printemps Qui Commence*?

W. B. Loud Glade

It must be morning – if that stain on the window pane be light. I am afraid I am suffering from Morning starvation, or it may be merely that I am exhausted after my decorous tantrum of yesterday in which I dealt with Aristotle, Hemingway, Sleep, W. B. Yeats, Einstein, and sundry other authors of fiction, organisers of faction. Some of these fine days I hope to present here the definitive appraisal of Yeats, for, by dad, fact it is that all critical matter already in print concerning him is of quite exceptional obtuseness and scandalous presumption. Moreover, the representation he is given in anthologies has caused to be disseminated a grotesque notion of the sort of mind he had, and what in heaven's name he was about at all. That I must change.

I wonder has there ever been an inspired misprint of the word YEATS, making it appear YEAST? Both, mind you, are noted for ebullience, for the capacity to transmute the base into the precious.

* * *

Yes, indeed, I was right – it *is* morning, still another of these matinal occurrences of downpour and freezing cold. My flunkeys have dressed me, reverently affixing my night shirt to a silver-plated coat-hanger. They have helped me into the fur coat, and from what I can see in the mirror, that green-inflected black object surmounting that assortment of delicate improvisations, the features which are ingeniously assembled to form my personal face, must be my County Manager's Hat. All this means I am going out somewhere, probably to give a lecture in Trinity on some theme of transcendent fatuity – maybe German verse, perhaps the *Goethesdämmerung*. Where is the car?

* * *

It is there. Before I can be helped into it I am approached by a healthy but alas! unfashionably dressed member of the beggar class. This fellow invokes blessings and benison on my head, of all places, before my bodyguard has had time to shoot him. (Why this passion for guarding my body I often wonder? Is the thing of some value? Is it a costly antique, a rate collector's piece? I must remember to have a word with Louis Wine about it.)

Well, here I am in the car, there are two secretaries in front with the brief-cases and the black hats and the two chauffeurs. How they all fit is a mystery the solution of which is of no interest. I am in the back with the doctor and his stethoscope, my stockbroker with the headphones and my personal frogman who is to make another attempt to find the Bowl of Light in the scabrous bed of the Liffey, and bring it to my house in Santry where it will be impounded, possibly even pounded.

We speed swiftly, skilfully avoiding the death-trap bollards with which the roads have been enrashed by the Corporation, and a weak signal is heard by all, that . . . life-rattle which is my way of speech indicates that I am dictating.

* * *

But let me here be the soul of candour. With hand upon my ♡, ladies and gentlemen, permit me to give the assurance that I am heartily sick of it all. How dearly I abhor all those things and people which Pliny called *cruditates qui nauseam faciunt*. The papers say that the City Hall crowd has devised a cabal whereby Dublin town is to be improved by an ingenious artifice whereby sixteen million pounds of rate-payers' money is to be spent. How nice that will be! I am sick of it all. Where are all the old crowd. Where is Harvey Duclos, Macredy the cyclist, Fred Jells, Cardinal Cullen, Hamar Greenwood, and Lord Aberdeen? Where is John Yeats, the grand portrait painter? *Where is Willie Yeats?* Ah, God be with the Celtic Twilight: it was not the worst. It reminds me of another thing, namely, the *Celtic Twilight*, which is the name of a book of essays W. B. Yeats published in 1893. I have it here and will now present a salutary quotation, for it deals with a character named 'Aristotle of the Books'.

The friend who can get the woodcutter to talk more readily than he will to anybody else went lately to see his old wife. She lives in a cottage not far from the edge of the woods, and is as full of old talk as her husband. This time she began to talk of Goban, the legendary mason, and his wisdom, but she said presently, 'Aristotle of the Books, too, was very wise, and he had a great deal of experience, but did not the bees get the better of him in the end? He wanted to know how they packed the comb, and he wasted the better part of a fortnight watching them, and he could not see them doing it. Then he made a hive with a glass cover on it and put it over them, and thought to see. But when he went and put his eyes to the glass, they had it all covered with wax so that it was as black as the pot; and he was as blind as before. He said he was never rightly kilt till then. They had him that time surely!'

I'll bet that was quare bee-loud glade, with a hive for the honey bee, and ever a welcome on the mat for Aristotle of the Books, Tarzan of the *Apes*.

Finnegan

There are those who say that *Finnegans Wake*, James Joyce's exode (that last word is copyright) is just a cynical leg-pull which he spent seventeen years in compiling; and there are others – and they vary from peasant-clerks in the State service here to the ex-G.I. type of literary scientist who festers in the over-endowed American universities – who allege it is the veritable apocalypse of the under-mind, a map of the floor of the soul, the anatomy of sleep and dream, a dissection of fate and destiny. The author's sudden death in 1941, amid the flux of war and only two years after publication of the book, did not enable him to entrust a wallet of clues about it to one of the numerous stooges who beset him, and those who like to look into the text now and again must not take it too seriously and must be content to think that they see things as if in a glass, very darkly.

Perhaps the infinity of meaning it can yield to bold inquirers is to be accounted a virtue – even if the crop be so disparate as to wear the accidents of fairyland and blasphemy. Joyce has been reported as saying that he asked of his readers nothing but that they should devote their lives to reading his works. Such a method of spending a lifetime would be likely to endow the party concerned with quite a unique psychic apparatus of his own. I cannot recommend it.

* * *

Many have thought it fortunate that *Ulysses* was anchored to Homer's epic in giving it a definite and predestined pattern. In the ballad 'Finnegan's Wake', Finnegan, a drunken navvy, falls off the scaffolding, smashes his skull and his body is hauled off to be waked at a ferocious hooley.

> Wid a gallon of whiskey at his feet
> And a barrel of porter at his head.

Later, when a different gallon of whiskey is fired at another guest, it misses, and falls all over Finnegan, who jumps up to prove he is alive all the time. No parallel of this happy ending can be discerned in *Finnegans Wake*, nor is the unpredictability of events isolated and studied. No, the material is a bit inconsequent. Perhaps an example will serve:

What Irish capital city (a dea o dea!) of two syllables and six letters, with a deltic origin and a numous end, (ah dust oh dust!) can boost of having (*a*) the most extensive public park in the world, (*b*) the most expensive brewing industry in the world, (*c*) the most expansive peopling thoroughfare in the world, (*d*) the most phillohippuc theobibbous paupulation in the world; and harmonise your *abecede d* responses? Answer: (*a*) Delfas.

As the Dublin man would say, you can make bacon out of that! What a prospect it must be to attempt a guide to such country – 'how paisibly eirenical, all dimmering dunes and gloamering glades, sellstretches afore us our fredeland's plain!' I say it with sorrow, but the reader can have my part of it and welcome.

*   *   *

The most recent psycho-palaeologist, exegetist, scholiast and cerebro-glottologist to take on the job, or part of it, is one Mrs Adaline Glasheen, whose *Census of Finnegans Wake* has just been published by Faber; on it is the sinister annotation 'Copyright by Northwestern University'. This is an identification of nearly all the many thousands of names in *Finnegans Wake*, a purported synopsis of the work which gets the reader nowhere at all, and a table setting forth 'Who is Who when Everybody is Somebody Else'. It is a thorough mess and really looks like a parody of this strictly American type of researching. Here is her handy definition of the book:

Finnegans Wake is a simulacrum of the world as the consciousness of man perceives it presented with good-tempered nihilism, without explanation or apology. It has no First Cause, only a First Riddler who may or may not know why a raven is like a writing desk. The riddle alone is real, the riddle and man's passionate desire to solve it.

Mrs Glasheen's five years of well-intended labour are blemished by many mistakes of reference and fact, and there are silly slips such as Cregan here and Creagan there and – heavens! – Myles na Copaleen here and Miles there. There is one curious bloomer. She gives the date of birth of Eamon De Valera ('not popular with Joyce') as 1822. The correct date is 1882. Know what that was? The year of Joyce's birth!

People in Books

I have been pondering an idea which, for re-pondering, I would recommend to the PEN Club. Unfortunately, it brings in question an obscurity in the law concerning copyright in literary property, and two books which I have consulted on copyright law give no help beyond continually stressing the general ambiguity of the statutes. (I wonder would those two doubt-infested books themselves be copyright?)

Some few things are clear enough. Under existing law, simple copyright in a literary work continues until after fifty years of the death of the author. Sir Arthur Conan Doyle died in 1930, and copyright therefore runs to 1980: an unauthorised re-issue of the Sherlock Holmes stories today would be unlikely to benefit the publisher. The stories are admittedly copyright but is Sherlock Holmes himself?

Does the law say that nobody else may now come forward with hitherto unpublished adventures by the great detective? It does not, so far as I can see. And if that is in fact the position, why cannot we now have those memoirs which he stipulated must not be made public until all the characters concerned, particularly that Cabinet Minister and the beautiful Countess L—— had been dead for forty years?

Your detective story-writer of today usually confronts his investigator with problems many times more fiendishly intricate than the worst which faced Holmes, but these writers are mere tradesmen, quite incapable of bringing to birth a great character like Holmes: their crimes are solved by fellows who are filled with sawdust, who never took a dart of cocaine in their lives. Why not turn their work over to Holmes?

* * *

This idea simply means that a skilled cook should buy trusted ingredients from a grocer before attempting to make a cake – unless, of course, the cook is so versatile as to *make* the ingredients as well as bake them. Few are. No considerations of copyright or punctilio, of course, prevents anybody from producing a few more volumes concerning Gargantua and Pantagruel, but those gentlemen's characters are imbedded in their doing inextricably, whereas Holmes is complete and detached, even if he had never gone out into the fog of Baker Street.

There is really nothing very new here. A person who takes in hand to complete a novel which its author left unfinished at his death re-energises the bereaved and stranded characters. Canon Sheehan left one such novel. And probably the best example is that of *The Mystery of Edwin Drood*, which many a man has tried to finish without result.

* * *

One is not so sure, of course, that other people's characters would not be more troublesome and headstrong than one's own, though it is true that one's own can sometimes get out of hand. Mr Patrick Kavanagh was writing a novel a few years ago, and I asked him how it was getting on.

'Divil a stir out of it for the last month,' he said. 'I got all those fellows into a field and I can't get them out.'

* * *

Are you a strict t.t.? says Joe.

Not taking anything between drinks, says I.

What about paying our respects to our friend? says Joe.

Who? says I. Sure, he's in John of God's off his head, poor man.

Drinking his own stuff? says Joe.

Ay, says I. Whiskey and water on the brain.

Come around to Barney Kiernan's, says Joe. I want to see the citizen.

Barney Mavourreen's be it, says I. Anything strange or wonderful, Joe?

Not a word, says Joe. I was up at that meeting in the City Arms.

What was that, Joe? says I.

Cattle traders, says Joe, about the foot and mouth disease. I want to give the citizen the hard word about it.

That's a damn dangerous damn thing, says I. You can get that off anything with croobs on it. Pigs.

You can get it off the fleas and bugs that do be buzzing off and on these animals and foostering about all over them – did you hear of a cow being washed or having a bucketful of carbolic thrun over it?

There's more than cows was never washed, Joe, says I.

I hope you only mean the citizen's dog and present company excepted, bar none. Come in here now.

There he is, says I, in his glory-hole with his cruiskeen lawn and his load of papers, working for the cause.

The bloody mongrel let in a grouse out of him that would give you the creeps. Be a corporal work of mercy if someone would take the life of that bloody dog. I'm told for a fact that he had a good part of the breeches off a constabulary man in Santry that came around one time with a blue paper about a licence.

Stand and deliver, says he.

That's all right, citizen, says Joe. Friends here.

Pass, friends, says he.

* * *

Then he rubs his hand in his eyes and says he:

What's your opinion of the times?

Doing the rapparee and Rory of the hill. But, begod, Joe was equal to the occasion.

I think the markets is in a state of collapse, says he.

So begob the citizen claps his paw on Joe's knee and he says:

Foreign wars is the cause of it.

It's the Russians want to tyrannise, says Joe.

Arrah, give over your bloody codding, Joe, says I. I have a thirst on me I wouldn't see for half a crown.

Give it a name, citizen, says Joe.

Wine of the country, says he.

What's yours? says Joe.

Ditto MacAnaspey, says I.

Three pints, Terry, says Joe, and we'll say a prayer and a half for that crowd of *glockauns* and *glooharawns* that makes me pay a bob for a pint.

You won't see them much longer, says the citizen, for home we will pack them in double-quick time and keep for ourselves what we own, the four green fields and the fair hills of Eire O. A shilling for porter, is it, a *wookul*? But whisper this much in my ear – who is to blame and what godbenighted imbeciles put them here or let them in at all? Who but ourselves may the Lord be merciful to us!

We'll kick them out all right, says I.

With your own kind assistance, citizen, says Joe.

We will indeed, *a cháirde* shouts the citizen. BUT CLOSE THE RANKS AND STEP TOGETHER! The friends we know are by our side, and the foes we hate before us!

Ah well, I might as well admit that that piece was written jointly by myself and Mr James Joyce, and we can do that sort of job fairly well, if we say it ourselves.

I've a better idea, though, the outline of which I will present here soon. I mean a play by Shakespeare with characters and speeches taken from several plays, and with a real plot which adds up. Hamlet kills Macbeth. Othello carries Ophelia away to the forest of Arden, Polonius marries Cleopatra, and suchlike carry-on.

Order your corpses in advance.

Dublin's Last Pub?

I mentioned Joyce yesterday. Now here is a little excerpt from *Ulysses*:

Mr Bloom ate his strips of sandwich, fresh clean bread, with relish of disgust, pungent mustard, the feety savour of green cheese. Sips of his wine soothed his palate. Not logwood that. Tastes fuller this weather with the chill off.

Nice quiet bar. Nice piece of wood in that counter. Nicely planed. Like the way it curves there.

Again:

His downcast eyes followed the silent veining of the oaken slab. Beauty: it curves: curves are beauty. Shapely goddesses, Venus, Juno: curves the world admires.

In charity I will not here name this pub. The liquor in it is good but physically it was transformed some years ago, on change of ownership into a sort of a . . . a shrine. That famous oak counter is quite gone. I wonder what happens when an ancient counter must make way for some fearsome vulgarity which is 'modn'? Perhaps they are donated to be made into replicas of ancient ships such as the *Mayflower*, or any similar manifestation of the awesome thing we may call whimsy. I hope so.

* * *

Now I want to change the scene to another famous Dublin pub. I take a great interest in pubs and their habituants. (What will you have?) The true pub *makes* its own customers. The nearest parallel I can think of is that of the religious orders: they are all very meritorious in themselves, but they earnestly dislike and despise each other. Did you ever see a Jesuit speaking to a Christian Brother? Right. Nor me. In Dublin's Harry Street, you have two pubs opposite each other, McDaid's and Mooney's. Both are very good houses *but I have never seen a soul who goes into one ever going into the other*. Don't ask me why: I simply do not know.

When I learned that this other famous Dublin pub had changed hands, I permitted myself a grimace of resignation. It would, of course, be eviscerated. That grand panelling would be ripped out, the shop's peaceful and sombre majesty electrified with hidden lights, the attendants trained to discuss the hydrogen bomb with anybody drinking gin, tonic and ice. And ah! – here the claw of fear truly numbed my heart – what about those magnificent gas lamps on the counter, great orbs poised on silver lamp posts, with gentle little gas mantles within them, casting on the gentle customary a gentle suffusion? They would walk, I said to myself sadly.

I began wondering how long it would take to bring the day when Dublin's last pub, embattled in its mahogany, and snugs and screens and private cubbies, would finally close, leaving the man who wants a drink nowhere to go but into one of the boudoirs known as 'lounge bars' or – worse – into some hotel where a fellow in a white jacket, having given you a look of contumely, draws across costly carpets a wagon loaded with *crème de banane* ekcetera from the central nest of which he contemptuously disinters your poor indigenous bottle of stout.

Eheu!

* * *

But be brave! There is a happy ending to this story. Not only did the new owner preserve the dignity of this old house but he has, with model taste, succeeded in adding to it.

Those magnificent gas lamps on the counter? They are still beaming as bravely as ever. Truly tasteful sets of pictures decorate the walls. The old atmosphere is intact. Mr Bloom would be quite at home. I congratulate the new owners, whose identity I have deliberately failed to ascertain.

In order to avoid a flood of inquiries, unaccompanied by stamped addressed envelopes, I may as well tell you that the pub is Neary's of Chatham Street.

AAAAHOOOO!

Do not, good reader, be intimidated by that spectacular title of mine. It is not just another dose of compulsory Irish. It is my attempt to represent a yawn.

Do not yawn at the idea of making the yawn the subject of a newspaper article. In the most mysterious scripture ever issued with the aid of public money – the Constitution of this, our 26-countied land – various 'rights' never heard of by most people are explicitly guaranteed. The Right to Yawn is not thus explicitly guaranteed, but apparently it is thought to be so fundamental as to be unmentionable. It proudly takes its place beside the Right to be Alive, the Right to Die, and the Right to go to the Bathroom in the Middle of an Argument which You Are Losing.

Last the Dáil of Erin met to consider, *inter alia,* a motion by Mr Jack Lemass, saying that the people of this country had no confidence in the Government of the day. As this newspaper reported, there was hardly anybody in the public gallery. The nation met Mr Lemass's challenge with a gigantic yawn. In emitting that yawn, they were doing no more than exercising a constitutional right. For all the good it done them!

* * *

The notion of people having any considerable interest in the spectacle of Feena Fayl scolding Fyn Gayl plus the Labourers' Party is mistaken. Insofar as the people – bemused body of inarticulate bystanders! – have any interest in contemporary politics, they ponder the choice that is given to the prisoner thus: 'You are going to die. Which would you prefer – a bullet through the head or be hanged?' Such a question evokes the etiquette of extermination. 'What would I look like as a corpse? Have I a right to be hanged in evening dress? Can I endow in advance a waiter with a few napkins to clear away the blood after they shoot me?'

Crudely translated, the problem is this: 'If we kick out the Present Crowd, what can come in except Your Other Men? And how many new grandmas, sons and daughters will we have to find jobs and pinshins for?'

Did you ever hear of a man who had seven grandmas, all encushioned in public employ?

I did.

* * *

That Constitution I mentioned is really a very funny document. The first time I saw it I was a bit startled at the indefeasible right given to disabled persons. Nobody, they were assured, could take away their right to meet 'peaceably and without arms'. That phrase presented myself with the vision of a great concourse in Dublin's College Green, standing by the jowl of the Old House – every man of them amputees – waiting for a blessing from the Chief, speeding toward them on the night train from Ennis.

Another day I hope to deal with this Constitution claws by claws. Article 40, for instance, is very good. It reads: 'All citizens shall, as human persons, be held equal before the law.' What is meant by this studied exclusion of inhuman persons? (Mind you, I have met a few of them in my time, every one of them owes me at least a fiver. I might agree that they should be jumped on, but putting them under a constitutional disability is bringing vindictiveness a bit far.)

Funnier or more sinister (take your choice) is Article 43. It says this: 'The State acknowledges that man, in virtue of his rational being, has the natural right, antecedent to positive law, to the private ownership of external goods.'

I suppose we all know at least one man who is not a man 'in virtue of his rational being'. Many of the recently deplored street accidents and fatalities arise from the necessity of crossing the street when you see him coming. But that bit at the end about 'external goods' is excellent. It amounts to an affirmation that no guarantee extends to the ownership of internal goods, and that those of us who fancy ourselves as the sole owners and beneficiaries of gastric or duodenal ulcers hug that delusion of ownership mistakenly. The Land Commission or some such body could take them off our hands overnight, at a nominal valuation!

Literature E'cet'ra

I am camping out! My house in Santry is in the hands of an army of workmen, being got ready for the Coronation, and I have betaken myself, with certain objects *de première necessité*, to exile in the Armoury – that strange building in the south-west corner of Santry Great Park, so familiar to Aer Lingus pilots.

The school? Hiberno-Byzantine, I should say. The part I call the *forum parvum*, got out in porphyry, Killaloe slates and the slobbers of several centuries of intemperate coachmen and gamekeepers, is stuffed with rifles and ammo. (No longer need we live and learn – in Larne, I mean!!!) The dome is there all right ('Say, that dome is floating!' an American once cried) with the usual pendetives and squinches; one of the great pillars has a slot in it, above the monogram 'M.R.', and all the letters posted here go down a mile into the earth via a chute lined with stainless glass. They will all be retrieved by some archaeologist in perhaps two thousand years hence – if hence two thousand be.

I do often post things there. I posted a poem of my own a week ago, plus a bundle of newscuttings about the milk strike cynically endorsed *udder times udder manners*. In the margin I had some notes on THE COW IN IRISH HISTORY, beginning with a disquisition on the *Táin Bó Cuailgne*, proceeding to such considerations as the word *bóthar* (road) being simply such track as will permit one cow to pass another, the Silk of the Kine, Clontarf or 'the bulls' meadow', the Red Cow Inn and so on, proceeding thence – fastidious exegete! – to a parallel with the Latin terms *pecus* and *pecunia*, and proving that the Romans came to Ireland after all!

I have the whole place whitewashed inside and out. And WHAT'S WRONG WITH THAT? Would you prefer blackwash?

No ruffyin such as Gropius or Lescaze nor any other bauhausboy will ever intimidate me. Those people say that the buildings they design are expressive of their age. Of their rage, they mean.

More betoken, I was sitting at the fire in the luxurious little pistolary (just off the torpedo gallery) last Sunday after dinner, and reflected that no novel expressive of our agues had been posted c/o Posterity. That was a shame, I told myself, as I rose to finger the treasures I had forninst me there. *The Small Mark, Dan,* by Maurice Walsh? No, too sentimental. O'Faolain's *A Curse of Paupers*? No, no, no – too much pessimism in that unfortunate man's head. I went through the lot and there wasn't a thing in the place that wouldn't LET US DOWN if you know what I mean.

If you do, let me in on it: I'm not too sure myself.

* * *

The result of this impasse was 4g1. If the job done to be was, I would have to do it myself (as usual). The vast canvas, of course. The false gold crust on life's sullen orb: the bronzed limbs of strong men whose stomachs are riddled with ulcers. Death. Women, slust – sluts, I mean. The whole works. I read somewhere recently about George Moore's sneer at Tolstoy for *War and Peace*, saying that he had tried to outdo Nature and would wake up screaming in the night: 'I forgot High Mass! I forgot a yacht race!' I intend to leave NOTHING out.

> There once was a writer of Santry,
> Who fed while he wrote in the pantry:
> If his books he found weighty
> From his too much potaty,
> Why, send into town for a gantry.

I got the typewriter, took the precaution of inserting a sheet of paper, and off with me. I progressed as far as page one, and on the way devised a very good pen-name. Here's p. 1:

THE HARD LIFE
A Study In Perfectionism
By Felix Kulpa

There was a knock – a toucher's knock, timidly brave. A certain thooleramawn came in.

'Ayn skayl noo?' I asked genially.

'Hope I'm not interrupting,' he said.

'Not at all. I was writing a novel, but I'm halfway through. I've the title page done. That's as much as the millions who read newspapers reviews and advertisements will ever see. It's the *vital* part of the job. I still have to write the book, of course, but . . . faugh! (*spits coarsely*) I could do that standing on your head.'

I gave this fellow a quid to buy an iron tonic for his sick mother and let him go. *Da quod jubes*, I muttered to myself, *et jube quod vis*.

* * *

I hold that all literature is, *per se*, disgusting. Turning a page is like lifting a flat stone – you see maggots. The most impermissible department of literature is poetry. The pretences are scandalous.

I see that the 'relaxation' of the new U.S. Treasury boss, Wilson, is 'detective stories'. That's *his* bash at literature. The night Attlee's crowd won the election I saw that he went home to his fire and became immersed in a whodunit. You see? We are expected to hold such creatures in awe. It is an extension of the theory that you cannot become a millionaire unless you left school at the age of four and sold newspapers in the streets.

There's a worse thing, though – and this goes mostly for poets. You might imagine that the vast international postal apparatus was devised for the purpose of transporting letters. Wrong. It was devised primarily to equip various 'literary' humbugs with old envelopes, carried in the inside pocket. I have never heard of a great work of art which was not 'written on the backs of old envelopes'. Have *you*? The poet should make his own of that business cliché – 'E.&O.E.' Ego and Old Envelopes.

* * *

I see where Paddy Kavanagh has been talking through his caub about this thing poetry. He says that the Gaelic poets thought writing poetry was easy. That is a very ignorant statement. In fact they were treated as Russians treat ballet dancers – they were snatched from their mothers' beasts (*stet*) at a tender age, put into beds in dark cells, and made to do nothing else for twenty-five years except learn to write the most intricate poetry imaginable. There was a lot of point in it though—THEY MADE A DAMN GOOD LIVING OUT OF POETRY AFTERWARDS. Those poets were born, not mad.

I noticed too, that there was a little tiff in junior school as to whether a man may permit himself to write poetry in a language which is not his native language. Poets are universally ignored, and it seems gratuitous to ensure being ignored the hard way. The thing is in questionable taste, too – it's like turning your back on your mother and marrying your aunt. (The Greek literateurs held that a man who does not marry his mother is no gentleman.)

The best plan is to write in one's own tongue for a strictly export market. Synge was perhaps the most monstrous phony and buffeon ever to enter our celtiç toilet, but he won international fame and money because foreigners extracted strange meanings and nuances from the language he used. Mr Joyce's *Ulysses* is very popular abroad, yet nobody but a Dublin Paddy could get more than ten per cent of its meanings: it is manifest that foreigners DO get meanings, but meanings which are other. *Compren*, eh? The magic of misunderstanding.

* * *

Practically anybody can write poetry, just as anybody can go to a dance in tails, white tie, plus fours, boots and bowler hat. It's all right if these things are done as a hobby or as a manifestation of harmless eccentricity. Now *here's* a defensible poem, for example:

> Two voices are there: one is of the deep:
> It learns the storm-cloud's thunderous melody,
> Now roars, now murmurs with the changing sea,
> Now bird-like pipes, now closes soft in sleep:
> And one is of an old half-witted sheep
> Which bleats articulate monotony,
> And indicates that one and two are three,
> That grass is green, lakes damp and mountains steep;
> And, Wordsworth, both are thine; at certain times
> Forth from the heart of thy melodious rhymes,

The form and pressure of high thoughts will burst:
At other times – Good Lord! I'd rather be
Quite unacquainted with the A B C
Than write such hopeless rubbish as thy worst.

That's a bit better than the work of palefaces who write
about Autumn, Love, Disillusion, the Hell of it All, and
that class of hopeless rubbish.

Who is the poet? That can be answered another day.

Records

Leinster House is a peculiar place. Its mere name is associated with Lord Fitzgerald. It connotes the propinquity of
rebellion. (Who said I couldn't invent a phrase?)

But Leinster House has been learning. The national
parliament has got to grips with the wire recorder. Three
deputies have wire recorders under the desk. They intend,
at the next meeting of the Committee of Public Accounts, to
demand to know why the official reporters are so inaccurate,
or why T.D.s are permitted to 'edit' their unwholesome
contributions. Leinster House resembles, not undistin-
guishably, Washington.

May I say something awful? Ministers of State in this
country are invited to get to work with the blue pencil on
their own remarks. They are given the opportunity for
second thoughts. They are invited to grow up. I believe that
they should be reported accurately, by the decent and honest
reporters who are employed for the job. Let the truth be
told though the heavens fall.

* * *

The wire recorder costs about £70. It can only be used in
any place where there is an electrical plug. It is noiseless in
operation. Those of us who were educated at Greyfriars
harbour an endemic contempt for the sneak, for the tale-
bearer. We automatically invite the overhearer to meet us
behind the ball-alley. Our aim is to give this unsavoury
person a hiding and a boxing lesson in one go. We wonder
how so dirty a personality can have as sister that lovely girl
Alice, who comes down on Prize Day.

'Take that, you cad!' we roar, as we fling a straight left to the point of the jaw. Thank heavens, there has not yet been any democratic nonsense in the management of those combats. We straight fellows always beat our man. We bloody his nose. Cries of 'Yaroooooh!' do not deter us.

This wire recorder is the instrument wherewith our code is being undermined. It involves a system of mechanical espionage. In a former day spies were shot at dawn. You cannot, however, shoot one of the machines I mention. Technically, it *can* be put out of order with bullets. But this process makes the executioners look ridiculous. The shooting detail will talk in the mess. 'The commandant is afraid of a gramophone. I have to be up at six in the morning to bump off one of them machines. And do you know what? One of the six of us is to have blank ammunition. Etiquette! And me a B.A. of U.C.C!'

* * *

Recently I called to see a friend of mine, a solicitor. I wanted his advice about a clear case of slander. I knew that the High Court would probably be most unsatisfactory, but felt that Conor Maguire would see me right at the heel of the hunt. This legal eagle said he would think about the content of my complaint and would let me know if I called back in the evening.

Call back I did. He said that before we got down to sordid business, he would give me a laugh. He produced a machine.

'Listen to this, for heaven's sake,' he said.

An appalling guttersnipe began talking out of the machine. The accent was *echt* Coombe. The recital was three-quarters over before I realised (from details of law-worthy woe sandwiched between various salacious anecdotes) that the speaker was I!

Never again! My traducer escapes.

Hunger Striking

I wish somebody would explain to me what exactly is the *theory* of the hunger strike. What is it intended to prove? What of the whyness of it? My inquiry is absolutely honest and I will be grateful for honest letters on the subject. If they are informative, I will return to the subject again. Self-immolation as some sort of public gesture seems to me primitive and pagan.

The Churches, particularly that severe one known as the Catholic, are united in condemning suicide. What is the difference between shooting yourself and starving to death? I discern none. A qualified theologian to whom I put the question bluntly said the hunger strike was a form of heroic protest, not necessarily fatal, and was therefore legitimate.

I asked him whether, when competent doctors had told a striker that the limit of his endurance had been reached, he was then bound by divine law to take nourishment. He evaded the question. How could human doctors know? How about supernatural nutriment?

I do not think that that sort of sophistry is funny. Those philosophers whom I watch so closely (called by the peasantry around Santry 'the angimals') will have none of your damn nonsense about hunger strikes. Fail to feed them three times daily at the appointed hour and they will roar the house down. They do not, of course, read the *Irish Times*. Perhaps that is just a little more evidence of their extreme cuteness.

* * *

This is a subject about which I speak with authority. A few weeks ago I had a serious intestinal disturbance, probably the result of having a meal in one of our Grade 'A' hotels. I hate talking about my bowels in public, but the national interest must be served. I did not send for a doctor because he would secretly look into one of the manuals he gets regularly from one of the three giant drug firms, and prescribe for me something he himself knew absolutely nothing about. With some vague thoughts of a passage in Cicero and a recent seeing of Pascal's film version of Shaw's *Androcles and the Lion* (in both locations simplicity is much praised), I decided that food was very bad for me and that I would discontinue its use for an indefinite time.

This experiment, if you like to call it that (I don't), lasted for one and a half days. It nearly killed me, I did not think that privation could be so bad. I began to suspect I would never be a real patriot of the heroic kind. It nearly killed me. What bothered me was not what we usually call hunger. If you are poor, you can get used to that. It was a situation of general paralysis. I could not think, read, work. Inexcusably, I forgot to feed a small dog I have. I did not intend that he should take part in my hunger strike. He approached me with his paw, suppliantly, looking for his dinner. He had a narrow escape. I nearly ett him.

* * *

There is an after-question to which I can get no answer either, from patriots or theologians. Hunger strikes are meaningless enough, but what would you say about a thirst strike? This means that you take nothing at all to drink, not even water. I have not tried it out in my personal experiments and do not intend to. But I do know that if you take no liquid for twenty-four hours, your body has already begun to rot. Within forty-eight hours the smell of putrefaction from you is terrifying, not to be compared with that of the monkeys at Shannon. You are yourself likely to be unconscious. You will undoubtedly be dead within four days. Just what in the lexicon of martyrdom prevents a hunger striker from being a thirst striker as well?

I am only basking, as the shark said.

This P.E.N.

Last Wednesday was quite a day in Dublin. I happen to know, because I was there and, furthermore, alive. I went along to the PEN meeting. I arrived late owing to obstruction of my bus by a hunger march staged by a section of our country's eighty thousand people who cannot get work and who don't emigrate because they can't find the fare.

Such an occurrence gives one paws, as remarked the broken-down actor when he confessed to his wife that he had landed the part of the cat in *Puss In Boots*. Why must plain people live in poverty when these 'literary' folk (who, to give them their due, don't appear to have any work either) can be flown from the ends of the earth to Dublin to talk damn nonsense in twelve languages when they are not guzzling free drink?

Nay, reader, think not that I complain, I merely express perplexity. Is a problem insoluble because it is ancient? The destitute and the leprous appear in the Christian story side by side with the Pharisees. Rarely has the pattern of human fate shed this (I hate this word but I'll use it) . . . this dichotomy, but I should like the PEN visitors to know that in Ireland we have achieved a trichotomy, for part of the obstruction which delayed my arrival was due to barricades of big new motor cars in the path of my bus. Here we have the poor, the tariff-sheltered rich, and the Fianna Fáil (present Government) Party.

I wish Peter Ustinov, one of our visiting PEN members, would let us have a letter on his views as to the proper management of our distressful political affairs. After all, didn't he burn down Rome in *Quo Vadis*?

* * *

Now here is a police message, which I print for the benefit of our PEN guests. If you buy, eat, or otherwise consort with Irish creamery butter in Dublin, you will find yourself in jail. *It is illegal!*

One does not adorn this solitary and terribly Irish fact. But fact it is and surely it is far more worth discussing than the theme of the conference – what can be done about people who write in obscure languages of limited orbit?

Military leaders are accustomed to mention the necessity for choosing between guns and butter, so why not have it out on the issue of books or butter? Yet my philosophic mind interrupts to remind us all that the eighty thousand people here who are workless do not worry themselves on this subject at all.

They eat a little margarine now and again.

* * *

Yet let us try to look on the bright side. The majority of the members of the Irish parliament are professional politicians, in the sense that otherwise they would not be given jobs minding mice at a crossroads. Yet simple people often have a peculiar sense of the fitness of things, as anyone travelling in rural Ireland will find out by asking for a drink of water at a cottage door. The caller will be told *you are going to have no drink of water, come in and rest yourself at the fire: Mickey, put that kettle on, Maggie, kill one of the turkeys immediately and here – sit down here – drink that up now, it's only a tumbler of dacent Irish whiskey and it won't do you a bit of harm because me husband, God rest him, never touched anything else!*

In honour of the PEN conference the good deputies, in parliament assembled, last Wednesday, spent the day discussing *a letter*. This letter, purportedly written by certain bishops in connection with the Health Bill, was circulated to several papers (though not to us) and thereafter utterly suppressed.

Why? I got my hands on a copy last Wednesday and saw nothing at all wrong with it. I hope to publish it next week after I have verified the soundness of certain references to canon law. But I thought the deputies' tasteful effort, in homage to PEN, to put it on the same level as the Ems Telegram or the Zinoviev Letter the sort of *curiosa felicitas* for which our peasantry may always be trusted.

*   *   *

Do you know what I think? I think this discourse of mine today is bad, *because we're nearly getting serious*! All the same, those marchers on Wednesday stuck in my mind long after hordes of policemen had headed them off to their tenements. I asked a fellow in a pub why it was that our president never gave a garden party for the unemployed. He had the cheek to reply that the Phoenix Park was too small.

I despise that sort of exaggeration.

But here's another rather theological speculation which came to me. Virtue and graces come from giving the goods of this world to the poor, as so many of the saints have actually done. What happens, spiritually, to the poor man thus enriched? Can he in turn earn merit by restoring this new-found wealth to his destitute benefactor. I aim at no facetious parallel about people perpetually taking in one another's celestial washing, but how can you give to the poor if you happen to be one of them, how can you deny yourself if there is nothing accessible to you wherewith yourself to deny?

I'm only asking.

*   *   *

The speakers at the PEN conference I found fascinating inasmuch as they seemed to me, notwithstanding how far they had come, replicas of our own branch of ineffectual sherry-drinkers. I can't quite remember what is the multiple significance of the initial PEN, but I think it is People, Poets, Poltergeists, Protestants, Paddies, Editors, Egotists, Ecbolicists, Eccentrics, Echoers, Ecstasists, Novelists, Neurologists, Nobodies, Nincompoops, Nuclearfissionmen . . . it really doesn't matter what they call themselves, it's what they ARE that matters.

How is that nobody has heard of the works of our distinguished visitors (I instantly concede that, God knows, we have heard enough about our own little brood)? I honestly begin to suspect that this PEN is an international Fianna Fáil party, in reality simply a junket, every man for himself, let everybody pay for our fun bar ourselves.

This much I *do* know. I moved heaven and earth and even Mars to get myself sent to a conference to a distant land as a fully paid-for delegate some years ago but there was nothing *because, forsooth, I was a communist*! What sort of an excuse is that, when we have had several communist delegates in Dublin, all armed with cameras?

*   *   *

I found the discussion about the future of people who write in obscure languages very naïve indeed, with its suggestion that great literary masterpieces are buried from the sight of eager humanity because they are written in a small language. If such a problem exists, why not turn back to our ancestors and our betters, despise vernacular tongues, and write in Latin? (I know the answer to that: very few of our friends of PEN can write or read Latin.)

But here, surely, is the master query about this PEN visit:

Why should Ireland be chosen as the rendezvous of an international society dedicated to the literary arts, since sundry illiterate and pietistical gangs have outlawed the circulation here of nearly all worthy books, by native as well as foreign authors? Why honour a country where political clodhoppers trample on people who own minds?

Why flatter peasants, instead of clearing off to America,

like Gogarty? Gogarty put swans on the Liffey to acknowledge his escape from country fellows with guns who tried
to kill him for speaking his mind. The PEN, it has been said,
is mightier than the SWORD. Is it? Remember, please, that
the mate of the PEN on the Liffey is the COB – and I am
going to be honest and admit I cannot remember which is
what sex.

So far as Ireland is concerned, let me assure our visitors
that here the CAUB is mightier than the PEN, and that
caub is an Irish word denoting the battered hat of the country
ruffian.

But don't mind me at all – shure I'm mad!

Protopolitics

How old is the science of politics in Ireland? Boys, but that's
a big question. A six-nark question, I would say. Assembly of
materials for the study of it would take a long time, a very
big hall, immense learning on the part of the querists, and
... *and* ... boundless patience. Do you remember the fearful
fuss some years ago when somebody discovered that one of
the politicians had got his own boots put into the National
Museum! Faith and that was the commotion! (I might here
confess that my own boots were also in the Museum at one
time – but I was inside them.)

It is a long time since it was discovered that real history
has little to do with dates and coronations and battles but
rather with social life and conditions, the price of bread, the
weather, the cast of men's minds. Very important is the
spiritual perception of an age. My own wide reading of what
remains of ancient Celtic documents impels me to the belief
that politics in Ireland were invented by a cabal variously
known as druids, poets, saints, advisers – a *gens* by no means
extinct, the sort of people who would leave far more than
their boots in the Museum.

*   *   *

One of the greatest poets in the period bordering on modern
Irish was named Eochaidh O Heodhusa (or O'Hussey), and
he too conceded that our ancestors believed in magic,

prayers, trickery, browbeating and bullying: I think it would be fair to sum that list up as 'Irish politics'.

One poem, edited many years ago by Eleanor Knott, takes my fancy, and I will try to convey it.

When the scene opens we see a group of thirty well-favoured T.D.s of nephological preoccupation. They are gazing at a cloud and in due course circulate word among the populace to beware of this cloud, to dig great shelters in the earth and shelter from it, because anybody struck by the moisture thereof would forthwith go off his rocker.

Here is one of O'Hussey's verses, but with my own weak gloss:

> *A shluagh an domhain, déanaidh*
> *uamha doimhne i ndroibhéalaibh*
> *(ar lucht eagna an bheatha bhí)*
> *ar eagla an cheatha ad-chluintí*

> Now listen, lads, please excavate
> Forbidding caves most tortuous
> (Thus warned those good interpreters)
> For fear this shower'll scorch us.

Crying wolf is an old hazard and the idea of being asked to build underground shelters by these professors just made the citizens laugh. It now began to get very dark and the brains trust thoughtfully retired to certain subterranean diggings of their own. The cloud swells, blackens, explodes and there is true desolation. Then the sky clears and my twenty technical men come up to the surface in the lift to say WETOLDYOUSO! Right enough, they saw that everybody who had remained out in the rain had gone stark mad. They were pleased at their own cuteness, but hold on till you hear what happened:

> *Gidh, eadh, do chuir cách i gcéill*
> *don bhuidhin úghdar ainnséin*
> *(dream dhreichmhíolla na ngníomh nglan)*
> *neimhchríonna dhíobh go ndearnadh.*

> The dauntless lads however conveyed
> To this assembled soggarthary
> (This beauteous band of peerless act) –
> That hiding was derogatory.

Déanaimne aimhghlic amhuil
sinn féin, ar na feallsamhain,
beag díol na cruinne dar gcéill
ná bíom 'san uile acht d'éinmhéin.

We must make batty just the same
Ourselves, the savants then opined:
Poor price the whole world for our wits,
If all men have not equal mind.

You see the extreme cuteness here? Your men realised
they had outsmarted themselves by remaining sane and
straightaway decided to make themselves mad, knowing the
mad majority would regard them as mad if they remained
sane. Here you have the genesis of all politician scheming.
(Don't overlook that phrase *sinn féin* in the third verse!)

Nbaslosm

There is no harm in an occasional fairy story by the fire. It
is no contradiction of that statement that what I have to tell
today is not a fairy story but absolute truth. It seems to be a
theological solecism to say that the truth can be ludicrous.
Parva est veritas? It is more than possible: I am beginning to
fear it is quite usual.

* * *

A friend called to my house early on Sunday morning and
invited me to accompany him to the bedside of another
friend who was ill. I was sitting alone, disconsolate, con-
templating a big fire which seemed to exude no heat. My
answer to the invitation was immediate.

No.

Why not? Are you sick or something?

I am not sick. As a matter of fact I am full of energy. But
I can't go out anywhere.

Why?

This morning, putting on my shoes, I broke the shoe-lace.
I tore the lace out of the shoe and threw it in the fire. It was
only then I discovered there was no spare shoe-lace in the
house. So I can't go out.

But surely you can get a lace from an old shoe? Wouldn't it last for the morning, anyway, for heaven's sake?

That is impossible. I have no old shoes.

Don't tell me you have only one pair of shoes?

I do so tell you. I discovered last year that shoe-repairing is a wasteful proposition. The proper soleing and heeling of a pair costs 12s 6d, often more. A cheap pair of new shoes can be had for twice that. My practice is to wear a pair until they become disreputable, or even water-logged, then throw them away and buy a new pair.

I see. Well, as an emergency measure . . . what about twine?

Twine? ME? Do you want old ladies to be giving me coppers in the street as a needy tramp? *Twine?*

* * *

Well, look – I've a car outside. Couldn't you get to the car, and then we could pull up somewhere and get a pair of laces. If you think that left shoe will fall off you getting to the car, couldn't you wear your slippers?

What slippers?

You don't mean to——

Yes I do. *Slippers!* Bah!!

Well . . . could I . . . carry you?

What was that you said?

Pardon?

Carry me, did you say? By gob I have enough trouble trying to do that meself. If that class of talk is meant to be serious, you're welcome to try – carry me with slippers on my croobs and bound with twine, but only on condition that we do it on the stage of the Theatre Royal, and not a penny less than twenty-five quid a week, and permission to slip across to O'Reilly's when the film is on.

* * *

Well, I'll end the *oratio recta*. What amounted almost to a show of force induced me to shamble to the car, keeping one foot on the ground, a gaunt spectre of a man, now saying to himself – *Aw, what the hell, didn't Hillary and Tensing get to the top of Everest?*

It is reasonable enough that the number and type of shop open on a Sunday is limited, but the awful discovery we made (time, about two hours, petrol cost, ten shillings) was that *you cannot buy a pair of shoe laces in Dublin city or south county on a Sunday.*

Hucksters, who had on sale everything from ladies' underwear to rubber stoppers for the exit route of bathwater, were all uniformly and apparently genuinely sorry. 'Ah, no, there's not a pair of gent's laces in the place.'

There was often the customary addendum: 'But I'll tell you where you might try. So-and-so's place, first turn on the right, it's a pub with a sort of another shop in it, you can't miss it.'

The pubs were not open at the time, of course. And imagine the indignity of a fine, or maybe a month, for being found on licensed premises within prohibited hours, charged with the illicit purchase, or attempted purchase, of a pair of shoe-laces.

The strange title of this piece is just an abbreviation: the letters stand for Never Break A Shoe Lace On Sunday Morning.

Down the Banks

Yesterday was held the annual meeting of the Cruiskeen Royal Bank of International Settlements and Dispensaries, Ltd. The Chairman, Sir Myles na Gopaleen (the da), having declared a dividend of twenty-eight per cent, said:

During the year under review, pressure of higher interest charges have been alleged to be detrimental to the re-issues of retained prior charges. This was not so. Account had not been taken, in this statement, of prior sub-charges and *contango* dealings. Annual drawings and the redemption value of the Bank's stock and Inner Resources, set aside to achieve equilibrium in times of monetary unbalance, had been offset by investments redeemable at fixed dates, and thus contraction in market prices had been provided against. It was noteworthy that the Bank's 'A' dealings in non-profit-bearing Gilt Edge had expanded.

The liquidity of sterling balances was a matter your Directors attended to with particular care. Assets standing at par had been redeemed but the resumption of bank credit had not been quite *pari passu* with gold and dollar reserves, whereas Government short-term borrowing in the nature of six-month bills had increased in disproportion to the national income. This was an economic infeasibility and would lead, unless the tendency was checked, to the re-issue, with a premium on par, of a spate of 'take-over' values sponsored by non-bank underwriting concerns. This tendency was looked upon with anything but equanimity by your Board; they had taken the step of putting a major investment into railway stock, the interest on which was guaranteed by public taxation.

'I want to make it clear,' Sir Myles said, with some feeling,

that the country is facing a crisis. There is a sinful and really scandalous shortage of productive effort. The balance of trade is chaotic. The farmers are so indolent that some of our smaller country towns are failing in their duty of conscientiously supporting four branches of separate banks. Some farmers, indeed, persons of dubious mental balance, have questioned the right of the bank clerks to escort their young daughters to all-night balls and other functions prolonged far into the dawn. Such aberrations accelerate the decay of rural life. They make Ireland once again the laughing stock of the world, and can lead to nothing but inflation.

Inflation was most important. It was a cancerous contamination of the monetary *corpus*. Profligate spending in Ireland, with no effort at simultaneous productivity, had seriously deflated the £ sterling, causing suffering and hardship to people – innocent people who had hurt nobody – so far away as Hong Kong. It was not a very Christian attitude and was one on which the Hierarchy was strangely silent. It was the duty of the Irish peasantry to work harder and spend . . . nothing at all.

I formally propose my own re-election as Chairman of the Bank and the payment of a dividend of twenty-eight per cent for the half year.

Shortly after the Chairman's proposals had been passed with acclamation, he moved freely among his fellow directors and senior shareholders, chatting genially and drinking malt. To an *Irish Times* correspondent he said: 'I know nothing at all about banking, but what is wrong with a half-year dividend of twenty-eight per cent? And my speech? You

must admit that I used the jargon as well as the rest of the
bank chairmen. Nobody can be accused of ignorance of
something that means nothing.'

Sir Myles then passed out.

Islanding

Some few weeks ago there appeared in this newspaper an
article under the head of 'The Islandman', by J. A. Brooks.
I wonder how many people read it with sympathy and understanding. The date was November 19th. The article took by
the scruff of the neck a subject I have, possibly through
caution, regarded for many years as a private grief. I knew
there was nobody to talk to about it. I regarded the book in
question with awe. (Not, as is customary, with 'Aw'.)

I read contemporary literature in five languages, thanks
to the Christian Brothers and an odd hiding now and again.
That book, *An t-Oileánach*, is the superbest of all books I
have ever read. Its sheer gauntness is a lesson for all. The
islandman starts with the concept that life is tough from the
cradle-view, and he is out gathering crabs to sustain his
betters before he is five. The man who wrote the remarkable
book, Tomás O Criomhthain, is dead, and the Great Blasket
is utterly deserted. Nothing now lives there except rabbits.

Mr Brooks says 'it is a nostalgic book'. So it is. It is the
symbol of a Gaelic order gone under for good. But it is an
extremely noble salute from them about to go away. From
another view, it is the apotheosis of native government. It
conforms in detail with the contemporary political jest of
having a Minister for the Gaeltacht. The lads are now gone,
their tongues at rest, their faces baked in salt water.

*   *   *

Mr Brooks in his article refers to the translation of *An
t-Oileánach* by the late Robin Flower as being 'a failure'.
Alas, Mr Brooks excels in charity, a charge never made at my
own door. A greater parcel of bosh and bunk than Flower's
Islandman has rarely been imposed on the unsuspecting
public. Not only was it a mistranslation but it gives a wholly
wrong impression, hiding inside its covers of opulent tweed.

Mr Brooks says that the book must be read in the original. I
applaud that outlook. The stranger is advised that it is worth-
while to learn the Irish language to read this work. Against it
about ninety per cent of books in English, with their smear
of sophistication, fall into the ordained bin of trash.

Mr Brooks also says the book is untranslatable. True
enough too, but I will attempt a short passage here, dealing
with the death of the author's mother:

The weather remained fine until I reached my mother in her
native retreat at Ventry – a long way from the Great Blasket,
between sea and land and, although there was a good funeral
turnout, plenty of carts and horses, it was on people's shoulders
that she went to the graveyard.

That was the end of the two who put the sound of this
language into my ears the first day. May God's blessing be on
them.

Most of us have to mourn the death of parents. But surely
to call them 'the two' is the utmost in legitimate pathos.

* * *

The book was published about 1930 and disturbed myself
so much that I put it away, a thing not to be seen or thought
about and certainly not to be discussed with strangers. But
its impact was explosive. In one week I wrote a parody of it
called *An Béal Bocht*. This prolonged sneer, long out of
print, will be republished shortly. My prayer is that all who
read it afresh will be stimulated into stumbling upon the
majestic book upon which it is based.

The Wood for the Trees

I wonder does it happen to other people, too? I mean the
obtrusion upon one's notice, for no reason at all, of some
thing, some circumstance in which one has no interest at all?
Something usually unpleasant?

If of a morning I narrowly escape being knocked down
crossing the street, it is a certainty that for the rest of the
day it will be one escape after another, with my Excellency's
survival growing ever more marginal and notional: all
wheeled transport will combine against me, even to the point

of disregarding the idea that the footpath was invented for feet.

If I buy a packet of cigarettes which turn out to be stale and unsmokable, I know it will be idle to throw them away and buy another packet; inevitably, the others will be staler.

Yesterday I was very nearly killed by a tree. An industrious householder was dismembering a massive beech which leaned over the public sidewalk, without any regard to the fact that I was passing by; a ton of timber had a very narrow escape from hitting me. When I reached the library of my place in Santry, I casually opened a book. I was confronted by that poem 'Trees' – perhaps the nastiest item of poesy ever contrived by the human brain; beside it the 'Inchcape Rock' and 'Lucy Gray' are masterpieces of subtle art. I opened the *Irish Times*. Yes, our London editor was not wanting: he complained that the Ministry of Works had felled many ancestral elms in Kensington Gardens because of a suspicion that they might fall on top of nursemaids.

*   *   *

While I was reflecting on this conspiracy, there was a ring at my door. A boy in blue handed in a cablegram. Where from, would you think? From Washington, of course. 'When your hands are idle . . .'

This sort of thing can be dangerous. A person who owns, as I do, an uninsurable cerebral equipment of unique precision and delicacy can take leave of his senses where there is a massive accumulation of this sort of 'coincidence'. I began to wonder just what sort of people plant trees. Was there some sinister communistic plot back of the fact that timber is measured in 'Petrograd standards'?

I tore open a letter which had been delivered that morning. It contained an examination paper set by the Civil Service Commissioners in connection with – honest! – appointments as Forestry Trainee.

The candidate was given twenty minutes wherein to rewrite what follows 'in your best handwriting with correct spelling and punctuation'.

O Connell was a yuneek personalitee no one like him had ever appeered at Westminster before and probablee no one like him will ever be scene their again he was best at stiring the feelings and arouzing the pashons his speaches were jeneralley punk-tyewayted by cheers and lahfter and anggry cries of dispewtayshon memorabl were his monnster open air meetings the gratest of them all was the mytee gatherring on the Hill of Tara every distrikt within sixtie miles of Tara sent kontingents to the meeting dewring the nite krouds with banners were konstantlee ariving to the meuzik of fyfes drums fiddls and bagpipes perfect order prevaled for miles on each side of every rode leeding to the hill were lines of veehekls of all kinds with the horses piketed in the adjoyning fields the resepshon of the Liberaytor was delirreus in its intensetee as his karrij proseeded up the hill the peepl greeted him with krys and eksklamayshons.

Well, I'm not going to make any more krys and ekskla-mayshons on this subject. I have just realised how pervasive, how circumambient is this stuff wood. When I am not standing on it, I am sitting on it. It is unavoidable.

An ignorant person may say: 'If you feel so strongly on the subject, why don't you kill yourself?'

That's not exactly the best way to avoid wood.